AF574980

WEBSTER'S DICTIONARY OF FIRST NAMES

WEBSTER'S DICTIONARY OF FIRST NAMES

Galahad Books • New York City

ISBN: 0-88365-492-X
Library of Congress Catalog Card Number: 80-85210

Contents

Introduction

Choosing a name is a very exciting and special experience. As an individual's hallmark, a name is more than just a means of identification.

Webster's Dictionary of First Names is an updated and complete compilation of both feminine and masculine first names. Each listing consists of a basic definition of the name, its place or language of origin, and any historical significance the name may have. Most commonly used American names are given, as are many of their foreign counterparts. Since certain names often may be spelled differently, multiple variations and diminutions are also included.

Divided into several sections, this dictionary also features a section where all the names included in the book are alphabetically listed for quick reference. There is also a special division where names not already listed can be placed.

Webster's Dictionary of First Names provides an interesting study of first names and their meanings, and can be a source of learning enjoyment and handy reference for any occasion.

DERIVATION AND MEANING OF MALE NAMES

A

Aaron (Hebrew) "mountain; light; higher strength." Also, in Hebrew, means "the enlightened or exalted one." Var. and dim., Aron, Haroun.

Abbot (Hebrew) "one who is father." Var., Abad, Abbe, Abbott, Abott.

Abel (Hebrew) "breath of vanity."

Abelard (Saxon) "one who is ambitious, resolute." Dim., Abbie.

Abiezer (Hebrew) "help of my father."

Abner (Hebrew) "lamp of the father; the son; of light." Dim., Ab, Abbie.

Abraham (Hebrew) "exalted father of the multitude." Var. and dim., Abe, Abie, Abram, Avram, Bram.

Adair (Celtic) "of the ford from the oak tree."

Adam (Hebrew) "man of the earth; from the red earth." Var. and dim., Ad, Adamo, Adan, Addam, Addis, Ade, Addy.

Addison (Saxon) "descendent of Adam."

Adiel (Hebrew) "the Lord's witness." Var., Adlai.

Adin (Hebrew) "one who is sensual; voluptuous." Var., Adan.

Adolph (Saxon) "the noble wolf:" from *Ead* meaning "happiness" and *ulph* meaning "help." Var. and dim., Adolf, Adolfe, Adolpho, Adolphus, Dolf, Dolph.

Adrian (Latin) "dark one; from the seacoast; from the city of Hadria." In Greek, also means "great or wealthy." Var., Adrien, Hadrian.

Alan (Celtic) "handsome, cheerful one; harmonious." Var. and dim., Al, Alain, Aland, Alano, Alayn, Allan, Allen.

Alban (Latin) "fair one; white." Var., Alben, Albin, Alva, Aubin.

Albert (Saxon) "noble, illustrious; all bright." Var. and dim., Al, Albie, Adelbert, Alberto, Aubert, Bert, Bertie, Elbert.

Alden (Anglo-Saxon) "old friend; wise protector." Var. and dim., Al, Aldin, Aldwin, Alwin, Elden, Eldin.

Aldo (Saxon) "rich; old or wise one." Dim., Al.

Aldous (Saxon) "the old one; one of the old house." Var., Aldis, Aldus.

Alexander (Greek) "one who protects mankind; helper." Var. and dim., Al., Alastair, Alec, Alessandro, Alex, Alexis, Allister, Sanders, Saunders, Sandy.

Alfred (Anglo-Saxon) "an elf; counselor; all wise or peaceful." Var. and dim., Al, Alf, Alfie, Alfredo, Fred.

Alger (Anglo-Saxon) "a spearman; noble one." Var., Algar.

Algernon (French) "one with whiskers." Var. and dim., Al, Algie, Algy.

Alphonse (Saxon) "a fighter or helper; one who is ready for battle." Var. and dim., Alfonso, Alonzo, Lon, Lonny.

Alston (Anglo-Saxon) "one from the old village or manor." Var. and dim., Al, Alton.

Alvin (Saxon) "one who is friend to all." Var., Alvin, Alwin, Elvin, Elwin.

Ambert (Saxon) "bright one; one who shines light."

Ambrose (Latin) "one who lives forever; immortal." Dim., Nam.

Amos (Hebrew) "one who is a burden."

Anatole (Greek) "one from the East." Var., Anatol.

Andrew (Greek) "manly one; one of strength." Var. and dim., Anders, Andreas, Andre, Andrien, Andy, Drew.

Angelo (Greek) "angelic, saintly one; a messenger." Dim., Angie.

Angus (Celtic) "one of strength; exceptional one." Dim., Gus, Gussie.

Anselm (Saxon) "helmet from God." Var., Anse, Ansel.

Anson (Anglo-Saxon) "son of the awe- inspiring Ann."

Anthony (Latin) "one beyond worth or praise." Var. and dim., Anton, Antoni, Antonio, Antony, Tony.

Archibald (Saxon) "sacred prince; bold one." Dim., Arch, Archer, Archie.

Arden (Latin) "one who is sincere, fervent." Also means "fiery, eager." Var., Ardin.

Argus (Greek) "vigilant one; guardian." Dim., Gus.

Arnold (Saxon) "one who is like an eagle; strong; mighty." Dim., Arne, Arnie, Arno.

Arthur (Celtic) "one with rock-like strength." Also, in Welsh, meaning "bearman." Var. and dim., Art, Artie, Arturo, Artus.

Arvin (Saxon) "one who is a friend of the people." Dim., Arv, Arvie, Arvy.

Asa (Hebrew) "physician or healer."

Asher (Hebrew) "one who is happy." Also, in Hebrew signifying "a boy who is quick to laugh."

Ashford (Anglo-Saxon) "one who dwells near the ash tree." Var. and dim., Ashley, Lee, Ashton.

Aubrey (French) "elf king; one who rules the elves." Also, in French, "a king whose blond hair formed a crown of gold upon his head." Var. and dim., Alberik, Bree, Brey.

August (Latin) "the exalted one; majestic." Var. and dim., Augie, Augus, Auguste, Augustine, Augustus, Austin, Gus, Gussie.

Averill (Anglo-Saxon) "one born in April." Also, "one who kills the wild boar," from Old English.

Avery (Anglo-Saxon) "one who rules the elves." Dim., Av.

Axel (Hebrew) "one who gives peace; father of peace."

Aylwin (Saxon) "awe-inspiring friend."

B

Baird (Celtic) "traveling musician; minstrel." Var., Bard.

Baldwin (Saxon) "courageous friend; protector." Var., Baldain, Baudoin.

Bancroft (Anglo-Saxon) "one from the bean field." In medieval times, "a bean grower."

Banning (Celtic) "little one with blond coloring."

Barnaby (Hebrew) "one who comes from prophecy; consolation." Var. and dim., Barna, Barnabas, Barney, Barny.

Barret (Saxon) "one with great strength; like a bear." Var., Barrett.

Barry (Celtic) "one who dwells at the barrier; spear."

Bartholomew (Hebrew) "one who plows or works the lands." Var. and dim., Barth, Bart, Bat.

Barton (Anglo-Saxon) "one who farms; worker of the land." Var. and dim., Bart, Barth.

Baructt (Hebrew) "one who is blessed." Var. and dim., Barrey, Barrie, Barry.

Basil (Latin) "one who is magnificent; a king."

Baxter (Saxon) "a baker." Dim., Bac.

Beau (Old French) "the handsome one."

Benedict (Latin) "the blessed one." Var. and dim., Ben, Bennett, Benny, Dixon.

Benjamin (Hebrew) "the son of the right hand." Var. and dim., Ben, Benjy, Bennie, Benson, Benny.

Benton (Anglo-Saxon) "one from the moors." Dim., Ben.

Berkeley (Anglo-Saxon) "one from the birch meadow." Var. and dim., Barclay, Berkley.

Bernard (Anglo-Saxon) "one who is brave as a bear." Var. and dim., Barn, Barnard, Barnet, Barney, Bernhard, Bernie, Bern.

Bertram (Latin) "brilliant raven; illustrious; a sign of wisdom." Var. and dim., Bartram, Bert, Bertie, Bertrand.

Bevan (Welsh) "son of the young nobleman." From *Ab-Evan* meaning "well-born." Var., Beavan, Beaven, Beven, Bevin.

Bing (German) "from the hollow."

Birkett (Middle English) "one who dwells in the birch land stretching before the sea." Var. and dim., Berk, Berkett, Birk.

Birley (Old English) "a byre on the meadow." Var., Berley.

Bishop (Old English) "the bishop."

Blade (Old English) "prosperous one; glory."

Blaine (Gaelic) "the one who is lean; thin." Var. and dim., Blain, Blane, Blayn, Blayne.

Blair (Gaelic) "of the place; of the field; plains."

Blake (Old English) "one with fair hair and complexion."

Blaze (Old German) "fiery torch; firebrand." Var., Blaise, Blase, Blayze.

Boden (Old French) "the messenger; heralder of news." Var., Bodan, Bodin.

Booth (Teutonic) "of the market; lover of home." Var. and dim., Both, Boot, Boote, Boothe.

Boris (Slavic) "strong warrior; able-bodied fighter; battler of tyrants."

Bowen (Celtic) "son of a well-born; descendant of Owen."

Boyd (Celtic) "one with fair hair; blond."

Brad (Anglo-Saxon) "of the broad place; wide."

Bradford (Anglo-Saxon) "of the wide river; the broad ford."

Bradley (Anglo-Saxon) "of the wide field; the broad meadow."

Bran (Celtic) "the raven; eternally young; symbol of youth."

Brant (Teutonic) "one of fire."

Brendan (Celtic) "from the mount of fire; beacon; shining bright light." Var., Brandan, Branden, Brandon, Brendon, Brennan.

Brent (Old English) "high sloping incline; steep."

Brett (Celtic) "one who comes from Brittany." Dim., Bret.

Brian (Celtic) "a strong leader with power and virtue." Var., Briant, Brien, Brient, Brion, Bryan, Bryant, Bryon.

Brice (Celtic) "sharp, quick-witted; one who is alert; ambitious." Var., Bryce.

Broderick (Teutonic) "descendant of mighty ruler who is renowned; one who is to rule." Var. and dim., Derick, Derrick, Roderick.

Bronson (Old English) "descendant of brown, darker one."

Bruce (Old French) "one who lives within the brushes; from the thickets."

Bruno (Teutonic) "the one with hair of brown color."

Buck (Old English) "one who is as swift and graceful as the deer." Var., Buckey, Bucky.

Budd (Old English) "the messenger and herald of kings and towns." Var. and dim., Bud, Budde, Buddie, Buddy.

Burgess (Teutonic) "one who dwells in the town; from the town." Var. and dim., Berg, Berger, Bergess, Burg.

Burke (Teutonic) "one who dwells within the stronghold; from the castle." Var. and dim., Berk, Berke, Bourk, Burk, Burkett.

Burl (Old English) "one who sears the cup of wine or mead." Var., Burle, Byrle.

Burton (Anglo-Saxon) "famous one; dweller in the protected village; of bright notoriety." Var. and dim., Bert, Berton, Burt.

Byron (Old French) "one who is from the country cottage; bear-like."

C

Cadmar (Welsh) "great and strong battle."

Cadmus (Greek) "one who adorns."

Caesar (Latin) "blue-eyed ruler; one with hair."

Caleb (Hebrew) "one who is faithful and bold." Sometimes meaning "dog" or "cow." Dim., Cal, Cale.

Calvert (Anglo-Saxon) "one who herds cattle." Var., Calbert.

Calvin (Latin) "one who is bald." Var. and dim., Cal.

Cameron (Celtic) "one who has a wry or crooked nose; one with individuality." Var. and dim., Cam, Camm.

Carey (Welsh) "one who dwells in castles; one who has a fortified home." Var. and dim., Cary.

Carleton (Germanic) "one who lives at Charles' town; one who dwells on a farm." Dim., Carlton.

Carlisle (Old English) "castle tower." Var. and dim., Carlyle.

Carroll (Celtic) "one who is manly; valiant champion." Var. and dim., Carel, Carol, Carole, Caryl.

Carson (Welsh) "son of the marsh dweller."

Carter (Anglo-Saxon) from a surname meaning "one who drives or makes carts."

Caspar (Persian) "a treasurer; keeper of the treasure; a horseman." Var. and dim., Casper, Cass, Cassy, Jasper, Kasper.

Cass (Latin) "one who is proud of his appearance."

Cassidy (Celtic) "a thinker or inventor; an ingenious person; curly-haired."

Castor (Latin) A name meaning "beaver."

Cato (Latin) "a cautious or careful person." Also means "wise."

Cecil (Latin) "one who is blind." Var. and dim., Cece, Cécile.

Cedric (Celtic) "a war-chief."

Chad (Anglo-Saxon) "fierce, with warlike tendencies."

Charles (Germanic) "one who is strong and manly." Var. and dim., Carl, Carlo, Carlos, Charley, Charlie, Chuck, Karl.

Chauncey (Latin) "a chancellor; official record-keeper." Var. and dim., Chance, Chancey, Chaunce, Chauncy.

Chester (Anglo-Saxon) "dweller in a walled town or camp." Dim., Ches, Chet.

Christian (Latin) "one who followed Christ." Dim., Chris, Christ, Christie.

Christopher (Greek) "a Christ-bearer." Var. and dim., Chris, Chrissy, Kester, Kit, Kris.

Clarence (Latin) "one who is bright; honorable or famous." Var. and dim., Clair, Clare.

Clark (Anglo-Saxon) "a clergyman or an intelligent, learned man." Var., Clarke.

Claude (Latin) "one who is lame." Var. and dim., Claud, Claudius.

Clayton (Anglo-Saxon) "one who is of earthly material or from a place of clay." Var. and dim., Clay.

Clement (Latin) "a merciful person." Var. and dim., Clem, Clemence, Clemente, Clim, Klemens.

Clifford (Anglo-Saxon) "one who dwells at the ford near the cliff." Dim., Cliff.

Clifton (Anglo-Saxon) "one who lives in a town or a farm near a cliff."

Clinton (Anglo-Saxon) "one who lives in a hill-town." Dim., Clint.

Clive (Anglo-Saxon) "cliff," or "cliff-dweller." Var., Cleve.

Clyde (Celtic) "one heard from a distance." In Welsh, also means "warm."

Coleman (Celtic) "a dove; keeper of doves." Var., Colman.

Colin (Celtic) "one who is strong and victorious; a pup or cub." Var. and dim., Colan, Cole.

Conan (Celtic) "one who has much wisdom." Var., Conant.

Conrad (Anglo-Saxon) "bold in speech and counsel." Var. and dim., Con, Connie, Cort, Curt, Konrad.

Constantine (Latin) "one who is firm or loyal." Var. and dim., Conn, Connie, Constant, Konstantin.

Corey (Celtic) "dweller in a ravine or mountain glen." Var., Cory.

Cormac (Irish) "a charioteer."

Cornelius (Latin) "hornlike; horn of battle." Var. and dim., Cornel, Cornell, Neal, Neil.

Corydon (Greek) "crested like a lark."

Cosmo (Greek) "of the world; orderly."

Courtney (French) "from the court or farmstead." Var., Courtenay, Courtland.

Craig (Celtic) "dweller of a mountain crag or stony hill."

Crosby (Anglo-Saxon) "of or near a crossroad." Var., Crosbey, Crosbie.

Curtis (Old French) "one who is courteous." Var. and dim., Court, Curt, Kurt.

Cuthbert (Anglo-Saxon) "one who is brilliant or illustrious." Dim., Cuddy.

Cyril (Greek) "one who is lordly." Var., Cyrille.

Cyrus (Persian) "one who is like the sun." Also refers to "throne." Var. and dim., Ciro, Cy, Rus.

D

Dacey (Celtic) "one from the South." Var., Dacy.

Dagan (East Semitic) "one who is like the earth or small fish." Var., Dagon.

Dagwood (Old English) "forest of the bright one."

Dalbert (Anglo-Saxon) "one who is proud and brilliant; bright valley; shining." Var., Delbert.

Dale (Anglo-Saxon) "one who lives in the valley." Var., Dalton.

Dallas (Celtic) "spirited one from fields of ravines; skilled one." Dim., Dal.

Dalton (Anglo-Saxon) "one from the valley estate."

Daly (Celtic) "one who gives counsel."

Damon (Greek) "the tame one; constant; domesticated." Var., Damian, Damien, Damion.

Dana (Anglo-Saxon) "a Dane; from Denmark." Var., Dain, Dane.

Daniel (Hebrew) "my judge is the Lord." Var., Dan, Dannie, Danny.

Darcy (Old French) "dweller of the fortress." In Celtic, refers to "dark." Var., Darsey, Darsy.

Darius (Greek) "one with great wealth; a king."

Darnell (Old French) "one who lurks in the secret place."

Darrell (Old French) "one who is beloved; dear." Var. and dim., Darryl, Daryl.

Darren (Celtic) "one who is small but mighty."

David (Hebrew) "the beloved one." Var. and dim., Dave, Davie, Davis, Davy.

Davin (Old Scandinavian) "of the Finns; alert; bright."

Dean (Anglo-Saxon) "of the valley." Var., Dene, Deane.

Delbert (Anglo-Saxon) "like the bright day." Var. and dim., Bert, Dal, Dalbert, Del.

Delmar (Latin) "of the sea." Var., Delmer.

Demas (Greek) "the dignified one."

Demetrius (Greek) "belonging to or loving the earth." Also, in Greek mythology, "belonging to Demeter, goddess of fertility." Var. and dim., Dimitri, Dmitri, Demmy.

Dempsey (Greek) "one who loves fine wines; a judge." Var. and dim., Denis, Dennison, Dennie, Denny, Denys, Denzil, Dion.

Dermot (Celtic) "one who is free." Var., Dermott.

Derrick (Anglo-Saxon) "one who rules the people." Var. and dim., Derek, Dirk.

Derry (Celtic) "one of red color."

Derwin (Old English) "friend who is beloved." Var. and dim., Darwin, Erwin.

Desmond (Celtic) "of the South." Also means "protector" in Anglo-Saxon. Dim., Desi.

Devin (Celtic) "one who writes verse (poetry)."

Dewey (Old Welsh) "one who is beloved."

Dewitt (Old Flemish) "one of blond coloring."

Dexter (Latin) "one who is right-handed." Also means "fortunate." Dim., Deck, Dex.

Dillon (Celtic) "one who is loyal; faithful."

Dixon (Anglo-Saxon) "one with Richard as father."

Dolan (Celtic) "black-haired one."

Dominic (Latin) "child born on the Lord's day." Var. and dim., Dom, Dommie, Dominick, Nick.

Donald (Celtic) "leader of the world; ruler." Var. and dim., Don, Donall, Donnell, Donnie, Donny.

Dorian (Greek) "one from or living near the sea (as in Doria, an ancient Greek city)." Var. and dim., Dim, Dore, Dorey, Dorien, Dory.

Douglas (Celtic) "one who lives near the black water." Var. and dim., Doug, Douglass.

Drew (Anglo-Saxon) "one of vision or skill; of wisdom and honesty." Var. and dim., Dru, Drue, Druce.

Dudley (Anglo-Saxon) "from the meadow of the people." Dim., Dud, Lee.

Duke (Latin) "one who leads the people."

Duncan (Celtic) "a dark one; a warrior." Dim., Dunc.

Dunstan (Anglo-Saxon) "one who dwells near the brown stone hill."

Durand (Latin) "one who endures." Var. and dim., Dante, Durante.

Durward (Anglo-Saxon) "one who guards or keeps the door." Var., Derwood, Durware, Durwood.

Dwayne (Celtic) "singing one." Also refers to "little one of dark coloring." Var. and dim., Duane, Dwane.

Dwight (Anglo-Saxon) "one of white or blond coloring."

Dylan (Old Welsh) "one from the sea."

E

Earl (Anglo-Saxon) "noble warrior or chief." Var. and dim., Earle, Erl, Erle, Errol.

Eaton (Anglo-Saxon) "from or of the river."

Ebenezer (Hebrew) "one who is a rock of help." Dim., Eb, Eben.

Edan (Celtic) "one like a flame."

Edgar (Anglo-Saxon) "lucky warrior; fortunate spear; prosperous." Var. and dim., Ed, Eddie, Eddy, Ned.

Edmund (Anglo-Saxon) "happy and prosperous protector; fortunate or rich." Taken from *Ead* meaning "blessed" and *Mund* meaning "peace." Var. and dim., Ed, Eddie, Eddy, Ned.

Edward (Anglo-Saxon) "prosperous guardian." Taken from *Ead* meaning "blessed" and *Ard* meaning "nature" or "disposition." Var. and dim., Ed, Eddie, Ned, Ted, Teddy.

Edwin (Anglo-Saxon) "fortunate friend." Taken from meaning "blessed" and *Win* meaning "conqueror." Dim., Ed, Eddie.

Egan (Gaelic) "one who is ardent; fiery; formidable."

Egbert (Anglo-Saxon) "the shining sword; bright." Var. and dim., Bert, Bertie.

Elbert (Teutonic) "one who is brilliant." Var. and dim., Albert, Bert, Bertie.

Eldon (Teutonic) "respected elder."

Eleazer (Hebrew) "one who is aided by God; help or court of God."

Eli (Hebrew) "the offering; highest." Var., Ely.

Elias (Hebrew) "the Lord, Jehovah, is God." Var., Elihu, Elijah, Eliot, Elliot, Elliott, Ellis.

Elisha (Hebrew) "the Lord is my salvation."

Ellery (Teutonic) "one from the adler trees."

Ellison (Hebrew) "descendant or son of Elias." Dim., Elison.

Elmer (Anglo-Saxon) "of noble fame; awe-inspiring." Var., Aylmer.

Elmo (Greek) "helmet; friendly protector."

Elmore (Anglo-Saxon) "one who lives at the moor of elm trees."

Elroy (Latin) "royal; the king." Dim., Eroy, Roy.

Elwin (Anglo-Saxon) "one who is friend to elves." Var. and dim., Elwyn, Winn, Wynn.

Elwood (Old English) "one of the old forest." Var., Ellwood.

Emanuel (Hebrew) "God is with us." Var. and dim., Emmanuel, Immanuel, Manny, Manuel.

Emil (Teutonic) "diligent; hard-working; industrious." Var., Emile, Emlyn.

Emmett (Teutonic) "industrious ant." Var. and dim., Em, Emmet, Emmy.

Emory (Teutonic) "ambitious leader." Var., Emery, Merrick.

Enoch (Hebrew) "dedicated; one who is devoted."

Ephraim (Hebrew) "growth; one who is fruitful." Dim., Ef, Efraim, Efrem, Ephrem.

Eric (Teutonic) "ever-kingly; powerful ruler." Var. and dim., Erich, Erik, Ric, Rick, Ricky.

Ernest (Teutonic) "vigor; honest intent; sincere." Dim., Ern, Ernie.

Erwin (Anglo-Saxon) "friend of the sea; sea-lover."

Esmond (Anglo-Saxon) "gracious protector; courteous guardian."

Ethan (Hebrew) "firm; one who is strong; steadfast."

Eugene (Greek) "well-born; noble." Dim., Gene.

Evan (Gaelic) "one who is well-born; youthful warrior." Welsh variation of John.

Everett (Anglo-Saxon) "always strong as the wild boar; honored."

Ezekiel (Hebrew) "my strength is God." Dim., Zeke.

Ezra (Hebrew) "the helpful one." Dim., Ez.

F

Fabian (Latin) "one who grows beans; wealthy farmer." Dim., Fabe.

Fairfax (Anglo-Saxon) "the yellow or fair-haired one."

Falkner (Anglo-Saxon) "one who trains or hunts falcons." Var. and dim., Faulkner, Fowler.

Farand (Teutonic) "one who is attractive; pleasant." Var. and dim., Farant, Farrand, Ran, Rand, Randy.

Farrell (Celtic) "one who is brave; valorous." Dim., Farell.

Felix (Latin) "the lucky, happy one; fortunate."

Ferdinand (Teutonic) "one who is bold; adventurous; daring." Taken from *Fred* meaning "peace," and *Rand* meaning "pure." Var. and dim., Ferd, Ferde, Ferdie, Fernand, Fernando, Hernando.

Fergus (Gaelic) "best choice of man; strong."

Firman (Anglo-Saxon) "distant traveler; strong."

Flavian (Latin) "the blond one; fair."

Fletcher (Teutonic) "one who feathers the arrows; arrowsmith." Dim., Fletch.

Flint (Old English) "the brook; stream."

Floyd (Celtic) "one with gray hair."

Flynn (Gaelic) "descendant of the man with red hair." Var., Flinn.

Forrester (Middle English) "guardian of the forests." Var. and dim., Forester, Forrie, Forster, Foss, Foster.

Francis (Latin) "a free man; liberated." Var. and dim., Fran, Francois, Frank, Franz.

Franklin (Teutonic) "a free man who owns land." Var. and dim., Francklin, Francklyn, Frank, Frankie, Franklyn.

Frederick (Teutonic) "peaceful ruler; chieftain." Var. and dim., Fred, Freddie, Freddy, Frederic, Fredric, Fritz.

Fremont (Teutonic) "one who is the free and noble protector."

Fulton (Anglo-Saxon) "one who is from the farm; of the place of game birds."

G

Gabriel (Hebrew) "man of God, who is my strength." Dim., Gabby, Gabe, Gabie.

Gabel (Old French) "the little Gabriel." Var., Gable.

Gale (Celtic) "energetic; lively one." Var., Gail, Gaile, Gayl, Gayle.

Galen (Greek) "wise healer." In Gaelic, the meaning is "precocious and bright child."

Galvin (Celtic) "shiny or bright white; sparrow." Dim., Vin, Vinny.

Gamaliel (Hebrew) "the Lord, God is my reward; recompense."

Gamel (Old Norse) "elderly; old."

Gannon (Gaelic) "little blond one; fair complexion."

Gardiner (Teutonic) "one who loves plants; gardener." Var., Gardener, Gardner.

Garfield (Old English) "field shaped like a triangle; triangular field."

Garland (Old English) "crowned with wreath of flowers; honored with a wreath of leaves; victorious." Var., Garlan.

Garett (Old English) "the brave spear; mighty spear." Var. and dim., Garet, Gareth, Garreth, Garrett, Garry, Garth, Gary, Gerard, Gerry, Jaret, Jary.

Garner (Teutonic) "noble guardian of the army; defender."

Garnet (Latin) "seed of the pomegranate; red jewel." Var., Garnett.

Garrick (Teutonic) "the great, mighty warrior; one who wields a spear well." Dim., Arick, Rick, Ricky.

Garvey (Gaelic) "difficult peace after much struggle."

Gary (Old English) "one who throws the spear." Var., Gari, Garey, Garry.

Gavin (Old Welsh) "one of the hawk field." Var., Gavan, Gaven.

Geoffrey (Teutonic) "God's peace throughout the land." Var. and dim., Geof, Geoff, Godfrey, Jeff, Jeffers, Jeffery, Jeffry.

George (Greek) "one who works the land; farmer." Var. and dim., Georges, Georgie, Jorge, Jorin, Joris, Jurgen.

Gerald (Teutonic) "mighty fighter and spearman." Var. and dim., Garold, Gereld, Gerrald, Gerry, Gery, Jer, Jerold, Jerrold, Jerry.

Germain (Teutonic) "one who is all victorious." Var., Germayn.

Gershom (Hebrew) "one who is exiled; new one in a foreign land."

Gervas (Teutonic) "honorable spear vassal; firm and sure." Var. and dim., Gervais, Gervase, Jarv, Jarvey, Jarvis, Jervis.

Gideon (Hebrew) "feller of trees; great, indomitable warrior."

Gifford (Teutonic) "present; gift; generous nature." Var. and dim., Giff, Gifferd.

Gilbert (Teutonic) "brilliant, shining promise; bright pledge. Taken from *Gisle*, meaning "a golden pledge." Var. and dim., Bert, Gib, Gibb, Gil, Gill.

Giles (Greek) from *aesidion*, meaning "kid, goat; bearded young companion."

Gilmore (Gaelic) "one who adheres to St. Mary." Var., Gillmore, Gilmour.

Gilroy (Gaelic) "he who serves the red-haired one."

Glen (Celtic) "he who resides in the valley." Var., Glenn, Glynn.

Goddard (Teutonic) "one who is as steadfast as the laws of God; firm." Var., Godard.

Godwin (Old English) "faithful friend of God; converted to God." Var., Goodwin, Goodwyn.

Gordon (Celtic) "big hill; triangular mount." Var. and dim., Gordan, Gorden, Gordie, Gordy.

Graham (Old English) "of the gray place or home." Var. and dim., Graeme, Ham.

Grant (Middle English) "one who is great."

Grayson (Middle English) "the reeve's son."

Gregory (Greek) "watchful one; he who keeps vigil." Var. and dim., Greg, Gregg, Gregor, Gregorie.

Griffith (Celtic) "strong chief; faith; red-haired one." Var. and dim., Griff, Griffin, Rufe, Rufus.

Griswold (Teutonic) "of the grey, wild forests."

Gunther (Teutonic) "brave fighter; bold."

Gustave (Scandinavian) "the staff of the nobles."

Guy (Teutonic) "the leader; warrior."

H

Hadden (Anglo-Saxon) "one who is from the valley of the heath." Var. and dim., Haddan, Haddon, Haden.

Hadrian (Latin) "a place of black soil; dark one."

Hadwin (Teutonic) "battle; companion."

Hagen (Celtic) "one who is little." Var., Hagan, Haggen.

Haines (Anglo-Saxon) "vine-covered cottage." Var. and dim., Hanus, Haynes.

Halbert (Teutonic) "one who is bright, noble." Dim., Hal.

Halden (Teutonic) "one who is half-Danish." Var., Haldan, Haldane, Haldin.

Hale (Teutonic) "a robust and sturdy man." Dim., Hal.

Halsey (Anglo-Saxon) "one who is from Hal's island." Dim., Halsy.

Halstead (Anglo-Saxon) "of the place of the manor house." Var., Halsted.

Hamilton (Anglo-Saxon) "the estate of one who loves his home." In French, means "one who is from the mountain."

Hamish (Hebrew) "may God protect; one who supplants."

Hamlet (Greek) "a small home."

Hamlin (German) "one who loves a small home." Var., Hamlyn.

Hamon (Teutonic) "a home." Dim., Hamo.

Hanley (Anglo-Saxon) "one who is from the high pasture." Var. and dim., Hanleigh, Henley, Henry.

Hannibal (Phoenician) "grace of God." Dim., Hanni, Hanno.

Hans (Hebrew) "gracious gift of Jehovah." In German, a shortened version of *John*.

Hansel (Scandinavian) "one who is a gift from God."

Harcourt (Teutonic) "the courtyard of the soldiers."

Harden (Anglo-Saxon) "one who is like a hare." Var., Hardan, Hardin, Hardunn.

Harding (Anglo-Saxon) "the son of a brave one."

Hardy (German) "one who is courageous." Var., Hardey, Hardie.

Harlan (Teutonic) "the land of armies or battles." In Old English, "a place where hares are plentiful." Var., Harland.

Harley (Anglo-Saxon) "the meadow of the hare or stag." Var. and dim., Arley, Arlie, Harl, Harleigh, Hart, Hartley.

Harlow (Anglo-Saxon) "a protected hill."

Harmon (Greek) "joining together; combining."

Harold (Norse) "powerful ruler or warrior; army." Var. and dim., Areldo, Hal, Harald, Harry, Herold.

Harper (Anglo-Saxon) "one who plays the harp."

Harrison (Teutonic) "one who is a son of Harry." Dim., Harri, Harris, Harrus.

Harvey (German) "one who will battle to protect his homeland." In French, means "bitter." Var. and dim., Harv, Harve, Hervey.

Hawley (Anglo-Saxon) "one who is from a hedged meadow."

Haydon (Teutonic) "one who is from an enclosed valley; hedged." Var., Hayden.

Hayes (Anglo-Saxon) "one who is a hunter."

Heath (Anglo-Saxon) "one who is from a wasteland."

Heathcliff (Anglo-Saxon) "one who is from the cliff of the wasteland."

Hector (Greek) "a steadfast defender." Dim., Heck.

Heman (Hebrew) "a faithful man." In Teutonic, "a soldier in the army."

Henry (German) "one who rules the home or estate." Var. and dim., Hal, Hank, Harry, Hendrick, Hendrik, Henri.

Herbert (Teutonic) "a bright warrior or army." Dim., Bert, Herb, Herbie.

Herman (Teutonic) "a man of high rank in an army." Var., Hermon.

Heywood (Teutonic) "one who is from a green forest." Var. and dim., Haywood, Woody.

Hezekiah (Hebrew) "the strength of Jehovah." Dim., Zeke.

Hilary (Latin) "one who is joyous; cheerful; merry." Var., Hilaire, Hillary, Hillery.

Hillel (Hebrew) "one who is praised greatly."

Hilliard (Teutonic) "a war-guardian."

Hilton (Anglo-Saxon) "from an estate of hills." Var., Hylton.

Hiram (Hebrew) "one who is exalted and noble; moral." Dim., Hi, Hy.

Hiroshi (Japanese) "one who is generous."

Hobart (Teutonic) "one of high intelligence; one who has a bright mind." Var. and dim., Bart, Hobbie, Hobie, Hobey, Hubie.

Holden (Anglo-Saxon) "one who is gentle."

Hollis (Anglo-Saxon) "one who dwells in the holly tree grove." Dim., Holl, Holly.

Homer (Greek) "a pledge or security." Var., Homere, Omero.

Horace (Latin) "one who marks time." Var. and dim., Horacio, Horatio, Horry, Race.

Hosea (Hebrew) "one of salvation."

Howard (Teutonic) "chief guardian or protector."

Howell (Welsh) "one who is alert and eminent."

Hubert (Teutonic) "one who has a bright mind; a genius." Var. and dim., Bert, Hube, Huberto, Hugh.

Humbert (Teutonic) "a bright giant." Also, "a bright home."

Humphrey (Teutonic) "guardian or protector of peace." Var. and dim., Humfry, Humphry.

Hyman (Hebrew) "life." Var. and dim., Hy, Hymen, Hymie.

I

Ian (Gaelic) "the Lord is gracious."

Ichabod (Hebrew) "where is the glory?; the glory has departed."

Ignatius (Latin) "the ardent, fiery one." Var. and dim., Ignace, Ignatz.

Igor (Scandinavian) "the hero."

Ingmar (Old Norse) "son of the famous one." Var., Ingemar.

Ira (Hebrew) "watcher; one with vision."

Irving (Old English) "friend of the sea." Var. and dim., Erwin, Irvin, Irvine, Irwin.

Isaac (Hebrew) "infant laughing when he was born; laughter." Var. and dim., Ike, Isaak, Iz, Izaak, Izzy.

Isidore (Greek) "present; gift from Isis." Var. and dim., Dore, Dorian, Dory, Isador, Isidor, Issy, Iz, Izzy.

Isaiah (Hebrew) "God is helper; salvation of the Lord."

Ishmael (Hebrew) "the Lord God hears."

Israel (Hebrew) "one who rules with God; prince of the Lord."

Ivan (Russian) "God's gracious gift." Russian for *John*.

Ivar (Scandinavian) "army bowman; archer." Var., Iver, Ives, Ivo, Ivon, Ivor, Yves.

J

Jaaziniah (Hebrew) "God-hears; the Lord answers prayer."

Jabez (Hebrew) "full of sorrow."

Jack (Middle English) English version of a Hebrew form of *John* meaning "gracious gift from God." Var., Jake, Jock, Jocko.

Jacob (Hebrew) "He who supplants." Var. and dim., Jacques, Jake, Jakie.

Jairus (Hebrew) "the Lord enlightens." Var., Jair, Jairis, Jayrus.

James (Hebrew) "supplanter; following after; one who replaces." Var. and dim., Hamish, Jacob, Jamesy, Jamie, Jem, Jemmie, Jemmy, Jim, Jimmie, Jimmy, Seamus, Shamus.

Japhet (Hebrew) "he who extends." Var., Japheth.

Jared (Hebrew) "the descendant; one who has longevity; luck."

Jason (Greek) "he who has healing powers."

Jasper (Persian) "brilliant, colorful gem." Var. and dim., Casper, Cass, Gasper, Kasper, Kass.

Jay (Anglo-Saxon) "lively bird."

Jed (Hebrew) From *Jedehiah* meaning "friend of the Lord; beloved of God."

Jeffrey (Teutonic) American spelling of *Geoffrey* meaning "peace." Var. and dim., Jeff, Jeffery, Jeffy.

Jeremy (Hebrew) "one who is exalted by the Lord." Var. and dim., Jeremiah, Jeremias, Jerry.

Jerome (Greek-Latin) From *Hieronymus* meaning "sacred name." Var. and dim., Gerome, Gerry, Jerry.

Jesse (Hebrew) "gift of the Lord; wealth; grace." Var. and dim., Jess, Jessie.

Jethro (Hebrew) "excellency; outstanding." Dim., Jeth.

Joab (Hebrew) "fatherhood."

Joachim (Hebrew) "the Lord judges."

Joel (Hebrew) "Jehovah is the Lord God; one who commands."

John (Hebrew) "the Lord is gracious; gift of God." Var., Evan, Gian, Giovanni, Hans, Ian, Ivan, Jack, Jan, Jevon, Jock, Johan, Johann, Johnnie, Johnny, Jon, Jonnie, Jonny, Juan, Sean, Shane, Shaughn, Shaun, Shawn, Zane.

Jonah (Hebrew) "dovelike; peace." Var. and dim., Jonas, Jone.

Jonathan (Hebrew) "gift of Jehovah." Dim., Jon.

Joseph (Hebrew) "one who increases; he shall add." Dim., Joe, Joey.

Joshua (Hebrew) "the Savior is God." Dim., Josh.

Josiah (Hebrew) "the Lord supports; fire of God."

Jotham (Hebrew) "the Lord God is perfect."

Judah (Hebrew) "the praise of God." Var. and dim., Judas, Judd, Jude.

Julius (Latin) "soft-bearded, youthful; divine." Var. and dim., Jule, Jules, Juley, Julian.

Justin (Latin) "virtuous; just; upright."

K

Kane (Gaelic) "small, rebellious one; tribute to bright, fiery, warlike boy."

Kay (Latin) "one who rejoices." Taken from *Sir Kay*, a knight from King Arthur's Round Table.

Keith (Gaelic) "one who is of the battlefield."

Kelly (Gaelic) "warrior of the king; brave soldier."

Keisey (Teutonic) "one who is of the ship-place; dweller by the water." Var., Kelcey.

Kenard (Anglo-Saxon) "benevolent nature."

Kendall (Celtic) "ruler of the valley."

Kenneth (Celtic) "one who is handsome; good-looking." Var. and dim., Ken, Kenney, Kenny, Kent.

Kenyon (Celtic) "one who has fair hair." Dim., Ken, Kenny.

Kermit (Celtic) "one who is a free man." Var. and dim., Dermot, Kerry.

Kerwin (Gaelic) "small one with jet-black hair." Var., Kerwen, Kirwin.

Kester (Old English) "one who is from the army camp of the Romans."

Kevin (Celtic) "handsomely born; comely; one who is gentle and lovable; kind." Var. and dim., Kev, Kevan, Keven.

Kimbal (Anglo-Saxon) "battlechief; ruler; warrior; royally bold; brave." Var. and dim., Kemble, Kim, Kimble.

Kirby (Teutonic) "from the church town; of the church village." Var. and dim., Kerby, Kerr.

Kirk (Scandinavian) "one who dwells near or resides at the church."

Konstantin (Latin) "one who is steady; firm."

Kyle (Gaelic) "he who is handsome." Also in Celtic, means "one who dwells by the chapel."

L

Lachlan (Gaelic) "the warlike one."

Lamar (Teutonic) "land-celebrated; renowned; popular."

Lambert (Teutonic) "wealthy in land; land-bright; brilliant." Var. and dim., Bert, Bertie, Lanbert.

Lamont (Norse) "one who studies law; lawyer; law-man." Var., Lamond, Lammond.

Lancelot (Anglo-Saxon) "the spear." Var. and dim., Lance, Lancey, Launce, Launcelot.

Langston (Anglo-Saxon) "one who is esteemed for his stature and property." Var. and dim., Landon, Langdon, Langley.

Lars (Scandinavian) "one who is crowned; victorious; celebrated with laurel crowns."

Larson (Scandinavian) "son of Lars."

Latimer (Anglo-Saxon) "one who translates or interprets the verse; teacher; one who masters language."

Lawrence (Latin) "crowned with wreaths of laurel." Var. and dim., Larrance, Larry, Lars, Laurance, Lauren, Laurents, Lon, Lonin, Loren, Lorenz, Lorenzo.

Lee (Anglo-Saxon) "from the pasture or meadow."

Leif (Scandinavian) "one who is well-loved; beloved."

Lemuel (Hebrew) "loyal to Jehovah; devoted; brilliant is the Lord God." Dim., Lem, Lemmie, Lemmy.

Leo (Latin) "lion; one who is as bold as a lion." Var., Leon, Lionel, Lyonel.

Leonard (Teutonic) taken from *Leon-hard* meaning "lion-brave." Dim., Len, Lennie, Lenny.

Leopold (Teutonic) "one who is patriotic; stands up for the people; brave or bold for the people." Dim., Leo, Lepp.

Leroy (Old French) taken from *le roi* meaning "the King." Var. and dim., Elroy, Lee, Leroi, Rex, Roy.

Leslie (Celtic) "of the gray fortress." Var. and dim., Les, Lesley.

Lester (Latin) "one who is from the army camp; chosen legion." Dim., Les.

Lewis (Teutonic) "celebrated warrior; renowned fighter." Var. and dim., Clovis, Lew, Lewes, Lou, Louie, Louis, Ludorick.

Lindsay (Old English) "the island of pools and linden trees." Var., Lindsey, Lindsy.

Linus (Greek) "refers to a boy with flaxen hair."

Lionel (Old French) "youthful lion; golden haired and brave."

Lloyd (Welsh) "gray; one with dark complexion; gray-haired." Var., Floyd.

Logan (Gaelic) "small hollow."

Lowell (Anglo-Saxon) "one who is loved; cherished; beloved."

Lucius (Latin) from *Lux* meaning "light;" Also, "an infant born at the break of day." Var., Lucian, Lucien.

Luke (Latin) "one who ushers in light, and hence, knowledge." Var., Lucas, Lucais.

Luther (Teutonic) "celebrated warrior." Var., Lothair, Lothar, Lothario.

Lyle (Old French) "one who comes from the isle."

Lyndon (Old English) "one who lives at the hill of linden trees." Var., Lindon.

M

Madoc (Celtic) "one who is kind and bountiful; beneficent; fortunate."

Madison (Teutonic) "one who is brave and bold in battle."

Magnus (Latin) "one who is great."

Major (Latin) "one who is a champion."

Malcolm (Scotch-Gaelic) "a disciple of St. Columbia."

Malise (Celtic) "a disciple of Jesus."

Mallory (Old French; Latin) "one who is ill-omened; the unfortunate one."

Malvin (Celtic) "a polished chief." Var., Melvin.

Manasseh (Hebrew) "one who is forgetful."

Manchu (Chinese) "one who is pure."

Manfred (Teutonic) "a peaceful man." Dim., Fred.

Manley (Teutonic) "one who is virile." Var., Manly.

Manuel (Hebrew) "God with us." Dim., Manny.

Manville (Latin) "from the large and great estate." Var. and dim., Manvel, Manvil, Mel, Melville.

Marcellus (Latin) "one who belongs to the god, Mars." Dim., Marcel, Marcelo.

Mario (Latin) "an offspring of Mars; one who is bitter or rebellious." Var., Marion, Marius.

Mark (Latin) "a warrior; an offspring of Mars." Var., Marc, Marco, Marcus.

Marlin (Anglo-Saxon) "one who is as cunning as a hawk." Var., Merlin, Marlon.

Marley (Anglo-Saxon) "one who is of the lake meadow."

Marlow (Teutonic) "from a hill by a lake." Var., Marlowe.

Marmaduke (Celtic) "a sea leader or steward." Dim., Duke.

Marmion (Gaelic) "one who is of sparkling fame."

Marsden (Anglo-Saxon) "one who is from the marsh." Var. and dim., Denny, Mardon, Marston.

Marshall (Old French) "a marshal or steward; an official in charge of the horses." Var. and dim., Marsh, Marshal.

Martial (Latin) "one who is warlike."

Martin (Latin) "warlike; an offspring of the god, Mars." Var. and dim., Mark, Mart, Marten, Martie, Martino, Marty.

Marvin (Teutonic) "famous; a friend of the sea." Var. and dim., Marv, Marwin, Mervin, Merwin, Merwyn.

Mason (French) "one who builds with stone."

Mato (American Indian) "one who is brave."

Matthew (Hebrew) "a gracious gift from the Lord." Dim., Mat, Mateo, Mathias, Matt, Mattias, Matty, May.

Maurice (Latin) "one who is dark; one who has black hair." Dim., Maury, Morrie, Morris.

Maximilian (Latin) "one who is the greatest; superior." Dim., Max, Maxim, Maxie.

Maxwell (Anglo-Saxon) "a large spring." Dim., Max, Maxie.

Mayor (Latin) "one who is the first in competition."

Maynard (Teutonic) "a powerful, mighty man; strength; firmness." Dim., Menard.

Meade (Anglo-Saxon) "one who is from the meadow." Dim., Mead.

Meredith (Celtic) "a sea protector or guardian." Var., Meridith.

Merle (French) "a blackbird; a dark-haired child." Var., Merl.

Meyer (Teutonic) "attendant or head servant to a king; a steward."

Micah (Hebrew) "like unto Jehovah; seeing."

Michael (Hebrew) "one who is like God; honorable." Var. and dim., Michel, Mickie, Micky, Mikael, Mike.

Miles (Latin) "a soldier." Var., Myles.

Millard (Anglo-Saxon) "one who flatters." Dim., Miller.

Milo (Latin) "a soldier; a merciful provider."

Milton (Anglo-Saxon) "from the mill-town or homestead." Dim., Milt.

Mitchell (Hebrew) "one who is like God; a spiritual man." Dim., Mike, Mitch.

Monroe (Celtic) "from the red swamp or marsh." Var., Monro, Munro.

Montgomery (French) "from the castles on the hill." Dim., Monte, Monty.

Montague (Latin) "of the peaked hill or mountain." Var., Montagu.

Morgan (Welsh) "a bright sea dweller; born by the sea." Var., Morgen.

Morley (Anglo-Saxon) "a pasture or meadow of ferns."

Morris (Latin) "dark-skinned; moorish." Var., Morice.

Mortimer (Latin) "one who is quiet; one who is like still water." In Celtic, the meaning is "sea warrior." Dim., Mort, Mortie, Morton.

Morton (Old English) "homestead by a marsh or moor." Dim., Mort, Morty.

Moses (Hebrew) "child saved from the water." Var. and dim., Moe, Mose, Mosie, Moss.

Murdoch (Celtic) "a prosperous protector of the sea." Var., Murdock, Murtagh.

Murray (Celtic) "a seaman." Also, in Middle English, means "merry." Var., Murry.

Myron (Greek) "fragrant or sweet oil." Var., Merrill, Myreon.

N

Nathan (Hebrew) "the Lord gave." Dim., Nat, Nate.

Nathanial (Hebrew) "a gift from the Lord God." Var. and dim., Nat, Natanael, Nataniel, Nate, Nathanael.

Neal (Gaelic) "noted warrior; winner; champion." Var., Neale, Neall, Neil, Neill, Nels, Niall, Nials, Niels, Niles, Nils.

Nelson (Celtic) "the descendant of Neal." Var., Nealson, Nilson.

Nicholas (Greek) "victorious people; those who conquer." Var. and dim., Claus, Colin, Klaus, Nichol, Nicholl, Nick, Nicky, Nicolas, Niles.

Nigel (Latin) "from Nigellas, meaning dark-complected and swarthy."

Noah (Hebrew) "comfort; repose; pause; to rest after travelling."

Noble (Latin) "one who is well-born." Var., Nolan.

Noel (Latin) "the day on which Christ was born."

Norman (Anglo-Saxon) "a norseman; man from the north." Dim., Norm, Normie, Norris.

Norton (Anglo-Saxon) "one who is from the northern estate."

O

Oakley (Anglo-Saxon) "of the oak-tree meadow."

Obadiah (Hebrew) "one who obeys the Lord; servant of God."

Octavius (Latin) "the eighth one." Var. and dim., Octave, Octavian, Octavus, Tavey.

Odell (Teutonic) "rich one; wealthy."

Ogden (Anglo-Saxon) "from the valley of oaks."

Olaf (Old Norse) "relic, ancestor; reminder of harmony and agreement." Var. and dim., Ola, Olin, Olini.

Oliver (Latin) from *Oliva*, meaning "'olive tree;' the symbol of peace; one who is benevolent." Var. and dim., Olivier, Ollie, Noll, Nollie, Nolly.

Omar (Arabic) "the highest; first born son; divine; richness."

Oren (Hebrew) "pine." Var., Orin, Orren, Orrin.

Orion (Greek) "son of fire-light." Var., Orian, Orien, Oryon.

Orson (Latin) "one who is like a bear; bear-like man." Var., Orsin, Orsine, Orsini, Orsino.

Orval (Anglo-Saxon) "spear-strong; one who wields the spear mightily."

Orvin (Anglo-Saxon) "one who is the spear companion."

Osbert (Anglo-Saxon) "perfectly brilliant; bright." Dim., Bert, Bertie, Berty, Oz, Ozzie.

Oscar (Anglo-Saxon) "perfect spear; spear-man." Var. and dim., Oskar, Ossie, Ozzie.

Oswald (Anglo-Saxon) "god-like power; divine force." Dim., Ossie, Oz, Ozzie.

Otis (Greek) "one who has an acute sense of hearing; keen hearing."

Otto (Teutonic) "one who is prosperous; rich; wealthy."

Ovid (Latin) "gentle guardian; benevolent leader; shepherd."

Owen (Celtic) "youthful warrior of noble birth." Var., Evan, Ewen, Owan.

Ozias (Greek) "the Lord is strong."

P

Page (Greek) "one who is attendant; chivalrous young attendant." Var., Paige.

Paine (Latin) "countryman; rustic; earthy." Var., Payne.

Palmer (Latin) "pilgrim who bears palms."

Parnell (Old French) "small; little Peter," Var., Pernel.

Patrick (Latin) "one who is honorable; noble; patrician." Var. and dim., Paddy, Pat, Partric, Patrik, Patty.

Paul (Latin) from *Paulus* meaning "little." Var., Pablo, Paulie.

Percival (Old French) "valley-piercer." Var. and dim., Perc, Perce, Perceval, Percy.

Perry (Anglo-Saxon) "tree that bears fruit; pear tree." Dim., Perr.

Peter (Greek) from *Petros* meaning "stone; rock." Var. and dim., Parnell, Pearce, Pedro, Pernell, Perrin, Pete, Petey, Petie, Petrie, Pierce, Pierre, Pietro.

Philip (Greek) "lover of horses." Var. and dim., Phelps, Phil, Phillip, Phillipi.

Plato (Greek) "one with broad shoulders; broad, large man."

Powell (Old Welsh) "descendant of Howell; Howell's son."

Preston (Anglo-Saxon) "from the place of the priest."

Q

Quentin (Latin) from *Quintus* meaning "the fifth-born child." Var. and dim., Quent, Quenton, Quint, Quinten, Quintin, Quinton.

Quillan (Gaelic) "youth; youngster; cub or buck."

Quincy (Gaelic) "one who resides at the estate of the fifth son."

Quinn (Gaelic) "one who is intelligent and wise."

R

Rad (Anglo-Saxon) "one who advises the ambassador."

Radcliff (Anglo-Saxon) "from the vermillion cliffs; dweller at the red cliffs."

Radolf (Anglo-Saxon) "one who counsels the wolves or warriors."

Ralph (Teutonic) "quick and agile wolf." Var., Rafe, Raff, Ralf, Rolf, Rolph.

Ramsey (Anglo-Saxon) "mighty, strong island; wooded island." Var., Ramsay.

Randolf (Saxon) from *Rand* meaning "shield" and *Wulf* meaning "wolf."

Raphael (Hebrew) "cured by the Lord God." Var., Rafael.

Raymond (Teutonic) "advised protection; wise shielder." Var. and dim., Ramon, Ramond, Ramone, Ray, Raymund.

Regan (Gaelic) "youth with title; young King or prince." Var., Raegen, Reagan, Reagen, Regen.

Reginald (Saxon) "strong; powerful; mighty." Var. and dim., Raynold, Reg, Reggie, Reggy, Reinhold, Reynold.

René (French) "one who is new again; reborn; rejuvenated."

Reuben (Hebrew) "behold, a son!" Var. and dim., Rube, Ruben, Ruby.

Rex (Latin) "king."

Rexford (Latin) "king's ford." Var. and dim., Rex, Rexferd, Rexfourd.

Reynard (Teutonic) "powerful." Also means "fox" in Old French. Var. and dim., Ray, Raynard, Reinhard, Reinhardt, Renard, Renaud, Rennard, Rey.

Rhett (Welsh) "full of enthusiasm." Var., Reece.

Richard (Teutonic) "strong ruler; wealthy." Var. and dim., Dick, Dickie, Dicky, Ric, Ricard, Ricardo, Riccardo, Rich, Richart, Richerd, Richie, Richy, Rick, Rickert, Ricki, Rickie, Ricky, Rico, Riki, Riocard, Ritch, Ritchie.

Richmond (Teutonic) "strong guardian; protector of the poor."

Rider (Old English) "equestrian." Var., Ryder.

Ridgley (Old English) "one who lives at the edge of the mountain meadow."

Ridley (Old English) "of the red field."

Riley (Gaelic) "courageous." Var., Reilly, Ryley.

Ring (Old English) "ring." Var., Ringo.

Riordan (Gaelic) "king's poet." Dim., Dan, Dannie, Danny.

Rip (Dutch) "mature; ripe."

Ripley (Anglo-Saxon) "from the field of the shouter." Dim., Lee, Leigh, Rip.

Roald (Teutonic) "notable sovereign; mighty."

Roarke (Gaelic) "famed sovereign." Var., Rorke, Rourke, Ruark.

Robert (Teutonic) "bright fame." Var. and dim., Bert, Bob, Bobbie, Bobby, Nob, Rab, Riobard, Rip, Rob, Robb, Robbie, Robby, Robers, Roberto, Robin, Robinson, Rupert, Ruperto, Ruprecht.

Rochester (Old English) "rocky citadel." Dim., Chester, Chet, Rock, Rockie, Rocky.

Rockwell (Old English) "from the rocky well."

Roderick (Teutonic) "noted lord; famous." Var. and dim., Broderick, Rick, Ricky, Rod, Rodd, Roddie, Roddy, Roderic, Roderich, Roderigo, Rodrick, Rodrigo, Rodrigue, Rodrique, Rory, Rurik, Ruy.

Rodman (Teutonic) "knight's aide; illustrious person; courageous; red-haired." Var. and dim., Rod, Rodd, Roddie, Roddy, Rodmann.

Rodney (Teutonic) "renowned." Dim., Rod, Rodd, Roddie, Roddy.

Roger (Teutonic) "illustrious lancer." Var. and dim., Rodge, Rodger, Rodgie, Rog, Rogerio, Rogers, Rudiger, Ruggiero, Rutger, Ruttger.

Roland (Teutonic) "from the land of fame." Var. and dim., Lannie, Lanny, Orlando, Rolando, Roldan, Roley, Rolland, Rollie, Rollin, Rollins, Rollo, Rolly, Rowland.

Romeo (Italian) "pilgrim to Rome; fame."

Ronald (Old Norse) "extraordinarily powerful authority." Var. and dim., Raghnall, Ranald, Renaldo, Ron, Ronnie, Ronny.

Rooney (Gaelic) "redhead." Var., Rowan, Rowen, Rowney.

Rory (Celtic) "red." Var., Rorie, Rorry, Rurik.

Roscoe (Old Norse) "from the deer forest." Dim., Ros, Ross, Rossie, Rossy, Roz.

Ross (Teutonic) "horse; peninsula; red." Var., Rossie, Rossy.

Roy (Latin) "king." Also means "red-haired" in Celtic. Var., Rey, Roi, Ruy.

Royce (Old English) "prince." Dim., Roy.

Rudolph (Teutonic) "famous wolf." Var. and dim., Dolf, Dolph, Raoul, Rodolf, Rodolfo, Rodolph, Rodolphe, Rolf, Rolfe, Rollin, Rollo, Rolph, Rudie, Rudolf, Rudolfo, Rudy.

Rudyard (Teutonic) "eminence." Also means "from the red enclosure" in Old English. Dim., Rudd, Ruddie, Ruddy, Rudy.

Rufus (Latin) "red-haired." Var. and dim., Griff, Griffeth, Griffin, Rufe, Ruff.

Russell (Latin) "red-haired." Also means "foxy" in Anglo-Saxon. Var. and dim., Rus, Russ, Russel, Rustie, Rusty.

Rutherford (Anglo-Saxon) "from the cattle ford." Dim., Ford.

Ryan (Gaelic) "prince."

S

Salvador (Latin) "of the Savior." Var. and dim., Sal, Sallie, Sally, Salvatore, Sauveur, Savior, Xavier.

Sam (Hebrew) "to listen." Var., Sammie, Sammy, Shem.

Samson (Hebrew) "sunlike; glorious; strong." Var. and dim., Sam, Sammie, Sammy, Sampson, Sansón, Sansone, Shem, Sim, Simpson, Simson.

Samuel (Hebrew) "requested; heard; name of God." Var. and dim., Sam, Sammie, Sammy, Samuele, Shem.

Sanborn (Old English) "from the sandy stream." Var. and dim., Sanborne, Sanburn, Sandy.

Sancho (Latin) "sacred; honest; earnest."

Sanders (Greek) "son of Alexander; helper of mankind." Var. and dim., Sanderson, Sandor, Sandy, Saunders, Saunderson.

Sanford (Anglo-Saxon) "living at the sandy ford." Var. and dim., Sandford, Sandy.

Sargent (Latin) "a military attendant; officer." Var. and dim., Sarge, Sargie, Sergeant, Sergent.

Saul (Hebrew) "requested; desired; longed for." Dim., Sol, Sollie, Solly, Zollie, Zolly.

Sawyer (Celtic) "woodcutter; woodsman." Var. and dim., Saw, Sawyere.

Saxon (Teutonic) "man of the sword." Dim., Sax, Saxe.

Schuyler (Dutch) "scholar; wise man; conceal; protector." Dim., Sky.

Scott (Latin) "from Scotland; tattooed." Var. and dim., Scot, Scotti, Scottie, Scotty.

Sebastian (Greek) "majestic; revered; beautiful." Var. and dim., Bastian, Bastien, Basty, Sebastiano, Sébastien, Sib.

Sedgwick (Teutonic) "victorious place." Var., Sedgewick, Sedgewinn.

Selby (Teutonic) "farm by the estate." Var., Shelby.

Seldon (Old English) "from the vale of willows." Var. and dim., Don, Donnie, Donny, Selden.

Selwyn (Teutonic) "friend of the mansion; forest; wild." Var. and dim., Selwin, Winnie, Winny, Wyn, Wynn.

Serge (Latin) "server." Var., Sergei, Sergio, Sergius.

Seth (Hebrew) "selected; appointed; substitute."

Seton (Anglo-Saxon) "from the coast."

Seward (Anglo-Saxon) "victorious guardian; defender of the seacoast." Var., Siward.

Sewell (Teutonic) "triumphant at sea." Var., Sewald, Sewall, Sewel.

Sexton (Middle English) "officer of the church."

Seymour (Old French) "from St. Maur"; Also means "sea-famous" in Teutonic; also "from the moor by the sea" in Old English. Dim., Morey, Morie, Morrie, Morry.

Shandy (Old English) "rowdy; unruly."

Shannon (Gaelic) "small; of wisdom."

Shaw (Anglo-Saxon) "resident of the grove."

Sheehan (Gaelic) "small; peaceable."

Sheffield (Old English) "from the uneven field." Var. and dim., Field, Fields, Sheff, Sheffie, Sheffy.

Sheldon (Anglo-Saxon) "from the ledge of the hill." Var. and dim., Shell, Shelley, Shelly, Shelton.

Shelley (Anglo-Saxon) "from the ledge or shelly meadow." Var. and dim., Shell, Shelly.

Shepherd (Anglo-Saxon) "tender of sheep." Var. and dim., Shep, Shepard, Shepp, Sheppard, Shepperd, Sheppy.

Sherard (Anglo-Saxon) "valorous; courageous." Var., Sherrard.

Sheridan (Celtic) "savage; wild." Dim., Dan, Dannie, Danny, Sherry.

Sherlock (Anglo-Saxon) "light-haired."

Sherman (Anglo-Saxon) "shearer of sheep; cutter of cloth." Dim., Man, Mannie, Manny, Sherm, Shermie, Shermy.

Sherwin (Anglo-Saxon) "loyal friend." Also

means "one who runs fast" in Old English. Var. and dim., Sherwynd, Win, Winnie, Winny.

Sherwood (Anglo-Saxon) "bright forest." Dim., Wood, Woodie, Woody.

Sidney (Old French) "from St. Denis." Var. and dim., Sid, Syd, Sydney.

Siegfried (Teutonic) "triumphant peace." Var. and dim., Siffre, Sig, Sigfrid, Siggy, Sigvard.

Sigmund (Teutonic) "triumphant guardian." Var. and dim., Sig, Siggie, Sigismond, Sigismondo, Sigismund, Sigismundo, Sigsmond.

Sigurd (Old Norse) "winning defender."

Silvanus (Latin) "woodland person; god of the woods." Var. and dim., Si, Sil, Silas, Silvain, Silvan, Silvano, Silvio, Sylvan, Sylvanus.

Silvester (Latin) "person of the woods; woodcutter." Var. and dim., Sil, Silvestre, Silvestro, Sylvester, Vest.

Simon (Hebrew) "hearer; obedient." Var. and dim., Si, Sim, Simeon, Siméon, Simone, Siomonn.

Sinclair (Latin) "saintly; illustrious light." Also means "St. Clair" in French. Dim., Clair, Clare, Sinc.

Skip (Old Norse) "ship captain." Var. and dim., Skipp, Skipper, Skippie, Skippy.

Sloan (Celtic) "warrior." Var., Sloane.

Smith (Old English) "blacksmith." Dim., Smitty.

Sol (Latin) "sun."

Solomon (Hebrew) "man of peace; wise." Var. and dim., Salmon, Salomo, Salomon, Salomone, Shalom, Sol, Sollie, Solly, Zollie, Zolly.

Solon (Greek) "sage."

Somerset (Old English) "from the summer place."

Spencer (Middle English) "provisioner." Var. and dim., Spence, Spense, Spenser.

Sprague (Teutonic) "alert."

Stacy (Greek) "one to be resurrected." Also means "reliable; wealthy" in Latin. Var. and dim., Stace, Stacey.

Stafford (Anglo-Saxon) "from the river crossing." Var., Staffard, Staford.

Standish (Old English) "stony grove."

Standfield (Old English) "rocky field."

Stanford (Old English) "stony river crossing." Dim., Ford, Stan.

Stanhope (Old English) "rocky valley."

Stanislaus (Slavic) "magnificent defender." Var. and dim., Stan, Stanislas, Stanislav, Stanislaw.

Stanley (Anglo-Saxon) "field of rocks." Also means "pride of the camp" in Slavonic. Var. and dim., Lee, Stan, Stanleigh, Stanly, Stannie.

Stanton (Anglo-Saxon) "from the stony place." Dim., Stan.

Stanwood (Anglo-Saxon) "rocky wood."

Stedman (Anglo-Saxon) "farm owner." Var., Steadman.

Stephen (Greek) "crown; garland." Var. and dim., Esteban, Etienne, Estevan, Stefan, Steffen, Stefon, Stephan, Stephanus, Steve, Steven, Stevie, Stevy.

Sterling (Teutonic) "truly valuable; real." Var., Stirling.

Sterne (Middle English) "severe." Var., Stearn, Stearne, Stern.

Stewart (Anglo-Saxon) "estate manager." Var. and dim., Stew, Steward, Stu, Stuart.

Stillman (Anglo-Saxon) "tranquil; peaceful; kind."

Stoddard (Old English) "person who tends horses."

Styles (Old English) "of the stiles."

Sumner (Latin) "caller."

Sutton (Anglo-Saxon) "from the southern place."

Swain (Teutonic) "young helper." Var., Swaine, Swane.

T

Tab (Old German) "drummer." Var., Tabb, Tabby.

Talbot (Old French) "bright as a valley; bloodhound; looter." Var. and dim., Talbert, Talbott, Tallbot, Tallie, Tally.

Tanner (Old English) "preparer of leather." Dim., Tan, Tann, Tannie, Tanny.

Tate (Teutonic) "full of cheer." Var., Tait, Taite.

Tavis (Celtic) "David's son." Also means "twin" in Gaelic. Var. and dim., Tav, Tavish, Tevis.

Taylor (Latin) "tailor." Var., Tailor.

Teague (Celtic) "poet; fair-skinned."

Tearle (Old English) "austere; harsh."

Tedman (Teutonic) "defender of the nation."

Templeton (Old English) "city of the temple." Dim., Temp, Temple.

Terence (Latin) "tender; tower-like." Var. and dim., Terencio, Terrence, Terry, Torrance.

Terrell (Teutonic) "warlike; thunderous ruler." Var., Terrill, Tirrell.

Thaddeus (Hebrew) "full of praise; brave." Var. and dim., Tad, Tadd, Taddeo, Taddeusz, Taddy, Tadeo, Thad, Thaddaus.

Thane (Anglo-Saxon) "king's follower; warrior." Var., Thaine, Thayne.

Thatcher (Anglo-Saxon) "one who thatches roofs." Var. and dim., Thacher, Thackeray, Thatch, Thaxter.

Thayer (Teutonic) "of the national army." Dim., Thay.

Theobald (Teutonic) "bravest prince of the people." Var. and dim., Dietbold, Ted, Tedd, Teddie, Teddy, Teobaldo, Thébault, Theo, Thibaud, Thibaut, Tibold, Tiebout, Toiboid, Tybalt.

Theodore (Greek) "gift of God." Var. and dim., Dode, Dore, Feodor, Feodore, Tad, Ted, Tedd, Teddie, Teddy, Teodor, Teodoro, Theo, Theodor, Théodore, Theodorous, Tudor.

Theodoric (Teutonic) "ruler of the people; people of power." Var. and dim., Derek, Derk, Derrick, Dirk, Dieter, Dietrich, Rick, Ted, Tedd, Teddie, Teddy, Tedric, Teodorico, Theo.

Theron (Greek) "a hunter."

Thomas (Hebrew) "a twin." Var. and dim., Massey, Tam, Tamas, Tammie, Tammy, Thom, Thoma, Tom, Tomás, Tomaso, Tome, Tomkin, Tomlin, Tommie, Tommy.

Thor (Old Norse) "thunder." Var., Thorin, Tor, Tore, Torin, Torre, Tyrus.

Thorald (Teutonic) "thunder's ruler." Var., Terrell, Thorold, Torald, Tyrell.

Thorley (Teutonic) "Thor's meadow." Var., Torley.

Thorndike (Old English) "from the bank of thorns." Var. and dim., Thorn, Thorndyke, Thornie, Thorny.

Thornton (Anglo-Saxon) "from the thorny village." Dim., Thorn, Thornie, Thorny.

Thorpe (Anglo-Saxon) "from the small town."

Thurlow (Old English) "from Thor's mountain." Var., Thorlow.

Thurman (Scandinavian) "protected by Thor." Var., Thorman, Thurmond.

Thurston (Scandinavian) "Thor's precious stone." Var., Thorstein, Thorsten, Thurstan.

Tiffany (Greek) "God's appearance."

Tilden (Anglo-Saxon) "from the rich valley."

Tilford (Old English) "from the productive ford."

Timothy (Greek) "worshiping God." Var. and dim., Tim, Timmie, Timmy, Timofei, Timoteo, Timothée, Timotheus, Tymon.

Titus (Greek) "giant." Also means "safe" in Latin. Var., Tite, Tito.

Tobias (Hebrew) "God is good." Var. and dim., Tobe, Tobia, Tobiah, Tobías, Tobie, Tobin, Tobit, Toby.

Todd (Latin) "the fox." Var. and dim., Tod, Toddie, Toddy.

Toland (Anglo-Saxon) "from land that is taxed."

Torrance (Gaelic) "from the ridges." Var. and dim., Tore, Torey, Torr, Torrence, Torrey, Torry.

Townsend (Anglo-Saxon) "from the end of town." Dim., Town, Townie, Towny.

Tracy (Latin) "brave fighter." Also means "reaper" in Greek. Var. and dim., Trace, Tracey, Tracie.

Trahern (Celtic) "with strength of steel." Dim., Tray.

Travers (Latin) "from the road crossing." Var., Traver, Travis.

Tremayne (Celtic) "from the place near the stone monument." Var., Tremain.

Trent (Latin) "stream with swift current."

Trevor (Celtic) "provident; judicious; circumspect; man of wisdom." Dim., Trev.

Tristan (Latin) "full of sorrow; harbinger; loud one." Dim., Tris.

Tristram (Latin) "unhappy task." Also means "intrepid" in Celtic.

Troy (Old French) "one who has curly hair." Also means "infantryman" in Gaelic.

Truman (Anglo-Saxon) "a faithful man."

Tucker (Old English) "a thickener or tucker of cloth." Dim., Tuck, Tuckie, Tucky.

Tully (Latin) "religious; serene; with God's peace." Var. and dim., Tull, Tulley.

Turner (Latin) "lathe-worker." Also means "tournament champion" in Old French.

Tybalt (Teutonic) "having capacity to lead people." Var. and dim., Theobald, Thibaut, Ty, Tybald.

Tyler (Anglo-Saxon) "maker of tiles or bricks." Var. and dim., Tiler, Ty.

Tynan (Gaelic) "dark." Dim., Ty.

Tyrone (Greek) "ruler with absolute power." Also means "land of Owen" in Irish. Dim., Ty.

Tyson (Teutonic) "son of the German." Also means "agitator" in Old French. Dim., Sonny, Ty.

U

Udell (Old English) "from the valley of the yew trees." Var. and dim., Del, Dell, Udale, Udall.

Ulric (Teutonic) "wolf-ruler; a strong, brave ruler." Var. and dim., Ric, Rick, Rickie, Ricky, Ulrich, Ulrick.

Ulysses (Greek) "full of anger; detester of dishonesty and injustice." Var., Ulick, Ulises.

Upton (Anglo-Saxon) "from the town on the hill."

Urban (Latin) "living in the city; worldly-wise; polite." Var., Urbain, Urbaine, Urbano, Urbanus.

Uriah (Hebrew) "the Lord is my light; light of God." Var., Urias, Uriel.

V

Vachel (Old French) "one who tends cows." Var., Vachil.

Vail (Anglo-Saxon) "residing in the valley." Var., Vale, Valle.

Val (Teutonic) "powerful; strong; mighty."

Valentine (Latin) "healthy; strong; valiant; a native of Valentia." Var. and dim., Val, Valente, Valentijn, Valentin, Valentín, Valentino, Valiant.

Valerian (Latin) "valiant; healthy; strong; brave; powerful." Var. and dim., Val, Valeria, Valerius.

Van (Dutch) signifies "of" or "from."

Vance (Dutch) "son of Van; thresher." Var., Van.

Varden (Celtic) "from the green hill." Var., Vardon, Verdon.

Varian (Latin) "changeable; intelligent."

Vaughn (Celtic) "small." Var., Vaughan.

Vere (Latin) "true; loyal."

Vernon (Latin) "springlike; youthful; thriving." Var. and dim., Lavern, Laverne, Vern, Verne, Verney.

Victor (Latin) "victorious; conqueror." Var. and dim., Vic, Vick, Vittorio, Vitorio.

Vincent (Latin) "conqueror." Var. and dim.,

Vicente, Vin, Vince, Vincente, Vincentius, Vincenty, Vincenz, Vinnie, Vinny.

Vinson (Anglo-Saxon) "son of Vincent; the conqueror's son."

Virgil (Latin) "bearer of rod or staff; thriving; strong." Var. and dim., Verge, Vergil, Virg, Virge, Virgie, Virgilio, Virgy.

Vito (Latin) "vital; alive." Var., Vite.

Vivian (Latin) "vigorous." Var. and dim., Viv, Vivien, Vyvyan.

Vladimir (Slavic) "prince of all; of royal fame." Var., Vladamir, Waldemar, Wladimir.

Volney (Teutonic) "spirit of the people; well-liked." Var., Volny.

W

Wade (Anglo-Saxon) "rover; living at the river crossing."

Wadsworth (Anglo-Saxon) "from the estate of Wade." Dim., Waddie, Waddy.

Wainwright (Old English) "maker of wagons." Dim., Wain, Wayne, Wright.

Waite (Middle English) "watchman; protector."

Wakefield (Old English) "wet field." Dim., Field, Wake.

Walcott (Anglo-Saxon) "walled cottage." Var., Walcot.

Waldemar (Teutonic) "famous sovereign; strong; powerful." Var. and dim., Valdemar, Wald, Waldimar, Waldo, Wallie, Wally.

Walden (Teutonic) "mighty ruler; from the forest."

Waldo (Teutonic) "powerful; ruler." Var. and dim., Wald, Wallie, Wally, Waldron.

Waldron (Teutonic) "powerful raven; authoritative."

Walford (Old English) "from the ford of the Welshman."

Walker (Anglo-Saxon) "cloth-thickener; walker of the forest." Dim., Wallie, Wally.

Wallace (Anglo-Saxon) "Welshman;

foreigner; stranger." Var. and dim., Wallache, Wallas, Wallie, Wallis, Wally, Walsh, Welch, Welsh.

Wallmond (Teutonic) "strong, protective ruler." Var., Walmund.

Walter (Teutonic) "powerful warrior; ruler." Var. and dim., Gauthier, Gualterio, Gualtiero, Gautier, Wal, Wallie, Wally, Walt, Walters, Walther, Wat.

Walton (Old English) "walled town; from the forest town." Dim., Wallie, Wally, Walt.

Ward (Teutonic) "guardian; watchman." Var., Warde, Warden, Worden.

Ware (Anglo-Saxon) "wary; wise; shrewd."

Warfield (Old English) "from the field by the dam."

Warford (Old English) "from the ford by the dam."

Waring (Latin) "true; cautious; protection."

Warner (Teutonic) "defense warrior." Var., Werner, Wernher.

Warren (Teutonic) "game warden; protector." Dim., Ware, Waring.

Warwick (Teutonic) "strong, protecting ruler; fortress." Var., Aurick, Vareck, Varick, Warrick.

Washburn (Old English) "from the flooded stream." Dim., Burn, Burnie, Burny, Wash.

Washington (Anglo-Saxon) "from the estate of the intelligent, discerning one." Dim., Wash.

Watson (Anglo-Saxon) "son of Walter."

Waverly (Old English) "from the field of wavering aspens." Dim., Lee, Leigh.

Wayland (Teutonic) "land by the road." Also means "workman" in Norse. Var. and dim., Land, Way, Waylen.

Wayne (Teutonic) "maker of wagons."

Webb (Old English) "weaver." Var., Weber, Webster.

Webster (Anglo-Saxon) "cloth-weaver." Dim., Web, Webb.

Welby (Scandinavian) "from the farm by the well."

Weldon (Teutonic) "from the hill spring."

Welford (Old English) "from the well by the ford."

Wellington (Anglo-Saxon) "from the rich man's mansion."

Wells (Old English) "from the springs."

Wendell (Teutonic) "traveler." Var., Wendel.

Wesley (Anglo-Saxon) "west meadow." Var. and dim., Lee, Leigh, Wes, Westleigh, Westley.

Westcott (Teutonic) "residing in the west cottage."

Weston (Old English) "from the western town." Dim., Wes, West.

Whitby (Scandinavian) "by the white village."

Whitelaw (Anglo-Saxon) "white hill."

Whitford (Old English) "of the white ford."

Whitney (Anglo-Saxon) "white island." Dim., Whit.

Whittaker (Old English) "resident of the white meadow." Dim., Whit.

Wilbur (Teutonic) "determined; brilliant." Also means "from the strong, loved castle" in Anglo-Saxon. Var., Wilbert, Wilburt.

Wiley (Old English) "wet meadow." Var., Wylie.

Wilford (Old English) "ford by the willows."

Wilfred (Teutonic) "determined maker of peace." Var. and dim., Fred, Freddie, Wilfrid, Will, Willie, Willy.

Willard (Teutonic) "firm; courageous." Dim., Will, Willie, Willy.

William (Teutonic) "firm protector; the helmet." Var. and dim., Bill, Billie, Billy, Guglielmo, Guillaume, Guillermo, Lyam, Vilhelm, Uilleam, Uilliam, Wilek, Wiley, Wilhelm, Wilkes, Wilkie, Will, Willem, Willet, Willi, Willie, Willis, Willy, Wilmar, Wilmer, Wilson, Williamson.

Willis (Teutonic) "son of William."

Willoughby (Anglo-Saxon) "by the willows."

Wilmer (Teutonic) "resolute; famous."

Wilmot (Teutonic) "determined mind; dearly loved."

Wilson (Teutonic) "son of William."

Wilton (Old English) "from the well of the town." Dim., Will, Willie, Willy, Wilt.

Winchell (Anglo-Saxon) "drawer of well-water; near a bend in the road."

Windsor (Teutonic) "at the river's bend; river boundary."

Winfield (Anglo-Saxon) "from the field of a friend." Dim., Field, Win, Winnie, Winny.

Winfred (Teutonic) "peace-lover." Var. and dim., Win, Winfrid, Winifred.

Winslow (Teutonic) "from the hill of a friend." Dim., Win, Winnie, Winny.

Winston (Anglo-Saxon) "friendly town." Var. and dim., Win, Winnie, Winny, Winton.

Winthrop (Teutonic) "from the village of a friend." Dim., Win, Winnie, Winny.

Wirt (Teutonic) "master." Also means "worthy host" in Anglo-Saxon.

Wolcott (Old English) "wolf's cottage."

Wolf (Teutonic) "wolf." Var. and dim., Wolfe, Wolfie, Wolfy.

Wolfgang (Old German) "advancing wolf." Dim., Wolf, Wolfie, Wolfy.

Wolfram (Teutonic) "wolf-raven; respected; feared."

Woodley (Anglo-Saxon) "from the meadow of many trees."

Woodrow (Anglo-Saxon) "from the woodland trail; hedgerow by the forest." Dim., Wood, Woodie, Woody.

Woodward (Anglo-Saxon) "warden of the forest."

Worth (Old English) "from the farmstead." Dim., Worthy.

Wright (Anglo-Saxon) "artisan of wood; carpenter."

Wyatt (Old French) "small warrior; guide." Var. and dim., Wiatt, Wye.

Wylie (Anglo-Saxon) "charming; pleasing." Var. and dim., Lee, Leigh, Wiley, Wye.

Wyman (Anglo-Saxon) "warrior."

Wyndham (Anglo-Saxon) "village reached by a winding path; windy village."

Wynn (Old Welsh) "fair one." Var. and dim., Winn, Winnie, Winny.

Wystan (Anglo-Saxon) "war stone."

X

Xanthus (Latin) "golden-haired."

Xavier (Arabic) "brilliant; splendid." Also means "new house" in Spanish Basque. Var., Javier, Xever.

Xenophon (Greek) "unfamiliar voice." Dim., Xeno, Zennie.

Xenos (Greek) "stranger."

Xerxes (Persian) "king." Dim., Zerk.

Ximenes (Spanish) form of *Simon*.

Y

Yale (Teutonic) "provider." Also means "corner of the land" in Old English.

Yancy (American Indian) "Englishman." Var. and dim., Yance, Yancey, Yank, Yankee.

Yates (Anglo-Saxon) "gate."

Yehudi (Hebrew) "praise of the Lord."

York (Latin) "sacred tree." Also means "estate of the boar" in Old English. Var., Yorke.

Yule (Anglo-Saxon) "December and January; Christmas child." Var., Yul.

Yves (Scandinavian) "bowman." Var., Ivar, Ives, Yvon.

Z

Zachary (Hebrew) "remembered by God." Var. and dim., Zacarias, Zacarías, Zaccaria, Zach, Zachariah, Zacharias, Zacharie, Zachry, Zachy, Zack, Zak, Zakarias, Zechariah, Zeke.

Zared (Hebrew) "ambush."

Zebadiah (Hebrew) "God's gift." Var. and dim., Zeb, Zebe, Zebedee.

Zebulon (Hebrew) "habitat." Dim., Lonny, Zeb.

Zedekiah (Hebrew) "God is mighty and just" Dim., Zed.

Zenas (Greek) "gift of God."

Zephaniah (Hebrew) "protected by the Lord." Dim., Zeph.

DERIVATION AND MEANING OF FEMALE NAMES

A

Abigail (Hebrew) "a father's source of joy." Var. and dim., Ab, Abbey, Abbie, Abby, Gael, Gail, Gale, Gayl.

Ada (Saxon) "joyous," or "prosperous." A depravation of *Eade*, an old Saxon name, signifying "happiness." Var. and dim., Addie, Addy, Aida, Eadith, Eda, Edith, Ida.

Adah (Hebrew) "ornament."

Adelaide (Saxon) "noble and of kind spirit." From *Adeliz*, the same as *Alice*. Var. and dim., Adalia, Adaline, Adela, Adele, Adelia, Adelina, Adelind, Adella, Adila, Dela, Della; plus all var. and dim. of Ada.

Adeline (Saxon) "noble; descending from nobles."

Adine (Hebrew) "gentle; delicate." Feminine form of *Adin*. Var., Adena, Adina.

Adora (Saxon) "the beloved; the adored."

Adrienne (Latin) "woman of the sea." Feminine of *Adrian*. Var., Adria, Adriana, Adriane, Adrianna, Adrianne.

Agatha (Greek) "good." Var. and dim., Ag, Agathe, Agathy, Aggie, Aggy.

Agnes (Greek) "pure; chaste; gentle." Var. and dim., Agna, Agnella, Nessie, Neysa.

Aileen (Greek) "light." Var., Alene, Aline, Eileen, Ilene, Iline, Illene, Illona.

Aimee (French) "beloved."

Alana (Celtic) "handsome or fair." Feminine of *Alan*. Var. and dim., Alana, Alina, Allana, Helen, Lana, Lane.

Alarice (Saxon) "ruler of all." Var., Alarise.

Alberta (Saxon) "noble and brilliant." Feminine of *Albert*. Var. and dim., Albertina, Albertine, Bert, Berta, Berte, Bertie, Elberta.

Alda (Saxon) "old" or "rich." A short form of *Aldith* in which the added syllable means "battle" or "war."

Aletheia (Greek) "truth." Var., Aletha, Alethea, Alethia, Alithea.

Alexandra (Greek) "helper of mankind." Feminine of *Alexander*. Var. and dim., Alexa, Alexis, Alix, Alla, Elexa, Sandi, Sandra, Sondra.

Alfreda (Saxon) "supernaturally wise." Feminine of *Alfred*. Dim., Ally.

Alice (Saxon) "truth" or "noble." Shortened from *Adeliz*. The French make it "defendress" by changing it to *Alexia* in their language. Var. and dim., Aleece, Alicia, Alis, Alisa, Alison, Alissa, Allis, Alyce, Alla, Allie, Ally, Alys, Elissa, Elsie.

Allegra (Latin) "cheerful; lively; merry."

Alma (Latin) "cherishing; loving; kind; bountiful."

Almira (Arabic) "princess; the exalted." Feminine of *Elmer*. Dim., Mira.

Alta (Latin/Germanic) "high" or "old."

Althea (Greek) "wholesome; healing." Var. and dim., Althee, Altheta, Thea.

Alva (Latin) "white; fair."

Alvina (Saxon) "beloved; friend of all." Feminine of *Alvin*. Dim., Vina.

Amanda (Latin) "lovable." Dim., Manda, Mandy.

Amber (Arabic) "jewel."

Amelia (Saxon) "industrious; striving." Feminine of *Emil*. Var. and dim., Amalia, Amelie, Mell, Mellie, Mill, Millie.

Amena (Celtic) "honest."

Aminta (Greek) "protect." Var. and dim., Amynta, Mindy.

Amity (Latin) "friendship." Var., Charity.

Amy (Latin) "beloved." From *Amata*. Var., Amee, Ami, Amie.

Anastasia (Greek) "one who will rise again; resurrection." Var. and dim., Ana, Stacey, Stacy.

Anatola (Greek) "of the East." Feminine of *Anatole*.

Andrea (Italian) "womanly." Feminine of *Andrew*. Var. and dim., Andee, Andi, André, Andreana, Andy.

Angela (Greek) "heavenly messenger" or "angelic." Var. and dim., Angel, Angelica, Angelina, Angeline, Angelita, Angie, Angy.

Anita (Hebrew) "grace." A form of *Ann* (originally Spanish). Var., Anitra.

Ann (Hebrew) "full of grace, mercy, and prayer." Originally from the name *Hannah*. Var. and dim., Anabel, Anabella, Anna, Anne, Annetta, Annette, Annie, Anora, Nan, Nana, Nancy, Nanete, Nanette, Nanine, Nanon, Nina, Ninette, Ninon.

Anthea (Greek) "like a flower." Var. and dim., Anthia, Bluma, Flora, Fleur, Thea, Thia.

Antonia (Latin) "super-excellent; a flower." Feminine form of *Anthony*. Var. and dim., Antoni, Antonina, Antoinetta, Antoinette, Netta, Nettie, Netty, Toinette, Toni.

April (Latin) "to open" (as the earth opens to renew itself in spring.)

Arabella (Latin) "fair and beautiful altar." Var. and dim., Ara, Arabelle, Bel, Bell, Bella, Belle.

Ardis (Latin) "zealous, bold, hardy, or fervent." Var., Ardelia, Ardelis, Ardella, Ardelle, Ardene, Ardine, Ardra.

Ariadine (Greek) "the holy one." Var., Ariadne, Ariana, Ariane.

Arlene (Celtic) "a pledge." Var., Arlana, Arleen, Arlena, Arlette, Arlina, Arline.

Astra (Greek) "starlike." Var., Astrea, Astred, Astrid.

Astrid (Norse) "divine strength."

Atalanta (Greek) "unswaying."

Athena (Greek) "one of wisdom." Var., Athene.

Audrey (English) "noble strength." Var. and dim., Audie, Audrie, Audry, Dee.

Augusta (Latin) "majestic; sacred." Feminine of *August*. Var. and dim., Augustina, Augustine, Austina, Austine, Gussie, Gusta, Tina.

Aurelia (Latin) "little golden dame." Var., Aura, Aurea, Aurel, Aurelie, Aurie, Aurora, Ora, Oralia, Oralie, Orel.

Aurora (Latin) "the dawn; the morning." As in *"Aurea hora,"* the golden hour.

Avis (Latin) "a bird." Var. and dim., Ava, Avi.

Aviva (Hebrew) "Spring."

B

Barbara (Greek) "mysterious foreigner; one of unknown origin; a barbarian; outlandish." Var. and dim., Babette, Babby, Babs, Barbette, Barby.

Beata (Latin) "divinely blessed." Dim., Bea.

Beatrice (Latin) "bringer of joy." Var. and dim., Bea, Beatrix, Bee, Trix, Trixie.

Belinda (Italian) "immortal and wise." In Italian it means "serpent." Dim., Bel, Linda, Lindie, Lindy.

Bena (Hebrew) "one of wisdom." Feminine form of *Benjamin*. Var., Benay.

Benedicta (Latin) "the blessed or the well-spoken one." The feminine of *Benedict*. Var., Benedetta, Benetta, Benita.

Bernadine (Saxon) "one of strength and courage." The feminine of *Bernard*. Var. and dim., Berna, Bernadette, Bernadina, Berneta, Bernetta, Bernette, Berni, Bernie.

Bernice (Greek) "bringer of victory." Var. and dim., Berenice, Berni, Berny.

Bertha (Saxon) "beautiful; bright and shining; famous." Var. and dim., Berta, Berti, Bertie, Bertina.

Beryl (Hebrew) "a precious jewel." Var. and dim., Berri, Berrie, Berry, Berryle.

Beth (Hebrew) "house of God."

Bethia (Celtic) "life." In Hebrew it means "Jehovah's daughter."

Beulah (Hebrew) "one who will be married."

Beverly (Anglo-Saxon) "one with great ambition." Var. and dim., Bev, Beverley, Beverlie, Bevvy.

Billie (Saxon) "willpower; resolution; a wise protector." Var., Bille.

Blanche (French) "white; fair, blond." Var. and dim., Bianca, Blanca, Blanch, Branca.

Blythe (Anglo-Saxon) "one of joy and happiness." Dim., Bliss, Blisse.

Bonnie (Latin) "sweet; pretty; good." Var. and dim., Boni, Bonita, Bonne, Bonni, Bonny.

Brenda (Saxon) "a sword; a fiery flame." Dim., Bren.

Brenna (Celtic) "a maiden with raven-black hair."

Bridget (Celtic) "mighty; fiery; strong." *Brighid*, in the Gaelic, also signifies "a hostage; a pledge of security." Var. and dim., Bridgid, Brie, Brieta, Brietta, Brigette, Brigida, Brigitte, Brita.

Brunhilde (Saxon) "battlefield heroine." Var., Brunhild, Brunhilda.

C

Calliope (Greek) "one with a beautiful voice."

Callista (Greek) "the most beautiful." Var. and dim., Calesta, Callie, Calysta, Kallista.

Camilla (Latin) "a noble and righteous handmaiden of unblemished character." Var. and dim., Cam, Camella, Camellia, Camille, Milly.

Candace (Latin) "glowing; fire-white; pure." Var. and dim., Candice, Candida, Candie, Candy.

Cara (Celtic) "a dear friend."

Carla (Saxon) "the strong one." The feminine of *Charles*. Var. and dim., Carlotta, Carly, Karla, Karly.

Carmel (Hebrew) "God's fruitful vineyard." Var., Carmela, Carmelita, Carmella.

Carmen (Latin) "one of song." Var. and dim., Carmena, Carmina, Carmine, Carmita.

Carol (French) "strong and womanly; joyous song." Var. and dim., Carey, Carole, Carolle, Carrie, Cary, Caryl, Karol, Karole.

Caroline (Saxon) "strong; little womanly one." A feminine form of *Charles* or *Karl* meaning "manlike and daring." Var. and dim., Carola, Carolina, Carolyn, Carrie, Karolina, Karoline, Karolyn, Lina.

Cassandra (Greek) "the entangling prophetess; one who inflames men with love." Var. and dim., Cass, Cassandre, Cassie.

Cecilia (Latin) "musical." Also means "gray-eyed, dim-sighted, or blind." Var. and dim., Cécile, Cecily, Celia, Cicily, Cis, Cissy.

Celeste (Latin) "heavenly." Var., Celesta, Celestine.

Celia (Latin) "heavenly."

Chandra (Sanskrit) "one who outshines the stars."

Charis (Greek) "full of grace."

Charity (Latin) "loving; generous; charitable." Var. and dim., Charita, Charry, Cherry.

Charlotte (Saxon) "a strong and noble woman." Another feminine form of *Charles*. Var. and dim., Carlotta, Charlene, Charline, Carry, Letty, Lotta, Lotte, Lottie, Lotty.

Charmaine (Latin) "little song of joy." Var., Charmain.

Cherie (French) "one who is cherished and dear; a sweetheart." Var., Cheryl, Sherri, Sherry, Shery.

Chloe (Greek) "fresh-blooming and verdant." In Greek it also means "young grass." Var., Cloe.

Chloris (Greek) "pale." Var., Cloris.

Christine (Greek) "fair breath of Christ." In Latin it means "Follower of the Anointed." The feminine of *Christian*. Var. and dim., Christa, Christabel, Christabelle, Christal, Christiana, Christina, Chris, Chrissie, Chrissy, Chrystal, Teena, Tina.

Clara (Latin) "clear; bright; shining or illustrious." Feminine of *Clarence*. Var., Claire, Clare, Clareta, Clarette, Clarine.

Clarabelle (Latin-French) "fair; bright; shining; beautiful." Var., Claribel.

Clarissa (Latin) "brightest or fairest; one who will be famous." Var., Clarice, Clarisa, Clarise.

Claudia (Latin) "the lame one." The feminine of *Claudius*. Var. and dim., Claude, Claudette, Claudie, Claudina, Claudine.

Clementine (Latin) "kind, gentle, merciful." Feminine of *Clement*. Var., Clementia, Clementina.

Cleopatra (Greek) "a famed father's glory." Var. and dim., Cleo, Cleona.

Clotilda (Saxon) "maiden of famous battle." Var., Clothilde, Clotilde.

Colette (Latin) "victorious one." Var., Collette.

Colinette (Latin) "little dove." Var., Columbine.

Colleen (Irish) "girl." Var., Coleen, Colene.

Constance (Latin) "firm and unyielding; unchanging; loyal." Var. and dim., Con, Conni, Connie, Conny, Constantia, Constantina, Constantine.

Consuela (Latin) "consolation-giver." Var. and dim., Connie, Consuelo.

Cora (Greek) "maiden." Var. and dim., Coralie, Corene, Coretta, Corette, Corinna, Corinne, Correna, Corrie, Corry.

Cordelia (Celtic) "daughter of the sea."

Cornelia (Latin) "queenly virtue; womanly; royal." Feminine of *Cornelius*. Var. and dim., Cornela, Nelia, Nell, Nellie.

Cymbeline (Celtic) "child of the sun."

Cynara (Greek) "artichoke."

Cynthia (Greek) "moon goddess." Dim., Cindy, Cyn, Cynth, Cynthie.

D

Dagmar (Danish) "joy of the land." Dim., Dag.

Daisy (Anglo-Saxon) "the day's eve; gay; cheerful." Var., Daisie.

Dale (Teutonic) "dweller in the valley." Var., Dail, Daile.

Dama (Latin) "lady."

Damaris (Greek) "a tree."

Daphne (Greek) "shy maiden of the laurel tree." Dim., Daph, Daphie.

Dara (Hebrew) "the heart of wisdom."

Darlene (Anglo-Saxon) "darling; dearly and tenderly beloved." Var. and dim., Darleen, Darline, Daryl.

Davina (Hebrew) "the loved one." Feminine of *David*. Var., Daveta, Davida, Davita.

Dawn (Anglo-Saxon) "the break of day."

Deanna (Latin) "bright as day."

Deborah (Hebrew) "like a bee; industrious." Var. and dim., Deb, Debbie, Debby, Debora, Debra.

Decima (Latin) "the tenth daughter."

Deirdre (Gaelic) "sorrowful one." Dim., Dee, Deedee, Deidre.

Delilah (Hebrew) "the temptress." Var. and dim., Dalila, Delia, Lila.

Della (Teutonic) "one of nobility." Dim., Del, Ella.

Delphne (Greek) "calmness; serenity."

Denise (Greek) "wine goddess." The feminine of *Dennis*. Var., Denice, Denys.

Desiré (French) "desire; salvation."

Diana (Latin) "virgin goddess of the moon." Var. and dim., Deanna, Deedee, Deni, Di, Diane, Dianna.

Dinah (Hebrew) "avenged."

Dione (Greek) "the daughter of heaven and earth."

Dixie (American) "a girl of the South." Dim., Dix.

Dolores (Latin) "our Lady of Sorrows." Var. and dim., Delores, Deloris, Dolora, Dori, Dorrie, Dorry.

Donna (Italian) "lady."

Dora (Greek) "a gift." Dim. of *Dorothy*.

Dorcas (Greek) "a doe, a roe-buck, a gazelle."

Dorene (French) "golden girl." Var. and dim., Doreen, Dori, Dorie, Dorine, Dory.

Doris (Greek) "goddess of the sea." Dim., Dodi.

Dorothy (Greek) "gift of God." A feminine form of *Theodore*. Var. and dim., Dee, Dolley, Dollie, Dolly, Dora, Dore, Doretta,

Dorothea, Dorothi, Dorthea, Dorthy, Dot, Dottie, Dotty.

Drusilla (Greek) "soft-eyed." Var. and dim., Dru, Drucilla, Drus, Drusie.

Dulcie (Latin) "charming; sweet." Var., Dulci, Dulcine.

E

Eartha (Anglo-Saxon) "the earth." Var., Erda, Erta, Ertha, Herta, Hertha.

Easter (Teutonic) from *Eostre*, the Anglo-Saxon goddess of spring, which was taken from *Eos*, the Greek goddess of dawn. Also, in religion, born at Eastertime. Var., Esther.

Ebba (Anglo-Saxon) "the return of the tide."

Echo (Greek) "repeated sound." In Greek mythology, the nymph *Echo* pined from unrequited love of Narcissus until only her voice remained.

Eda (Anglo-Saxon) "happy; wealthy." Var. and dim., Edda, Edie.

Edana (Celtic) "zealous; fiery." Feminine of *Edan*.

Eden (Hebrew) "delightful; pleasant; typifying femininity." Var., Edin.

Edina (Teutonic) "wealth; friendship; happiness."

Edith (Teutonic) "rich gift; tall; stately" Also means "the lady" in Saxon. Var. and dim., Dita, Eadie, Eadith, Eda, Ede, Edi, Edie, Edina, Edita, Editha, Edithe, Ediva, Edna, Edy, Edyth, Edythe, Eyde, Eydie.

Edlyn (Anglo-Saxon) "noble one; princess." Dim., Lyn.

Edmonda (Anglo-Saxon) "wealthy protector." Feminine of *Edmund*. Var., Edmonia, Edmunda.

Edna (Hebrew) "rejuvenation; pleasure; delight." Dim., Ed, Eddi, Eddie, Eddy, Edith, Edny.

Edrea (Hebrew) "mighty." Also means "powerful; prosperous" in Old English. Var. and dim., Eddi, Eddie, Eddy, Edra, Edrena.

Edwardine (Anglo-Saxon) "wealthy guardian." Feminine of *Edward*.

Edwina (Anglo-Saxon) "prosperous and valued friend." Feminine of *Edwin*. Var. and dim., Eadwina, Eadwine, Edina, Edwine, Edwyna, Win, Wina, Winnie, Winny.

Effie (Greek) "esteemed; fair; famed." Var. and dim., Effy, Eppie, Euphemia, Euphémie, Phemie.

Eglantine (Old French) "sweetbrier rose; woodbine."

Eileen (Greek) "light." Irish form of *Helen*. Var., Aileen.

Elaine (Greek) "light." French form of *Helen*. Var. and dim., Alaine, Alayne, Elana, Elane, Elayne, Laine, Lainey, Lane, Lani, Layney.

Elata (Latin) "lofty; triumphant; beautiful."

Eldora (Spanish) "golden one."

Eldrida (Anglo-Saxon) "wise counselor."

Eleanor (Greek) "light." Var. and dim., Eileen, El, Elaine, Eleanora, Eleanore, Eleanour, Elena, Elenor, Eleonora,

Eleonore, Eléonore, Elianora, Elinor, Elinore, Ella, Elladine, Elle, Ellen, Ellene, Elli, Ellie, Ellinor, Elly, Ellyn, Elna, Elnora, Elnore, Elora, Elyn, Helen, Leanor, Lena, Lenora, Lenore, Leonora, Leonore, Leora, Nelda, Nell, Nellie, Nelly, Nora.

Electra (Greek) "brilliant; shining star." Dim., Lectra.

Elena (Greek) "light."

Elfrida (Anglo-Saxon) "elfin; good counselor." Feminine of *Alfred*. Var., Elfreda, Elfride, Elfrieda.

Elga (Teutonic) "holy."

Elise (Hebrew) "oath of God." Var., Eliza, Elyse, Elysia.

Elissa (Saxon) "true; noble." Var., Alissa, Elisia.

Eliza (Hebrew) "oath of God." Dim., Liza, Lizzie.

Elizabeth (Hebrew) "dedicated to God; gracious; ambitious." Var. and dim., Babette, Belita, Belle, Bess, Besse, Bessie, Bessy, Beth, Betsey, Betsy, Betta, Bette, Betti, Bettina, Bettine, Betty, Ealaside, Eilis, Elisa, Elisabet, Elisabeth, Elisabetta, Elise, Elissa, Eliza, Elizabet, Elsa, Elsabet, Elsbeth, Else, Elsey, Elsi, Elsie, Elspet, Elspeth, Elsy, Elyse, Helsa, Isabel, Lib, Libbey, Libbi, Libbie, Libby, Lisa, Lisabet, Lisabeth, Lisbeth, Lise, Lisette, Lissa, Liz, Liza, Lizabeth, Lizbeth, Lizzie, Lizzy, Lusa, Tetty, Ysabel.

Ellen (Greek) "light." Var. and dim., Elena, Elin, Ellene, Ellie, Ellin, Elly, Ellyn, Elyn, Nell, Nellie.

Ellice (Hebrew) "Jehovah is God." Feminine of *Elias*.

Elma (Greek) "amicable; great fame." Feminine of *Elmo*.

Elmira (Teutonic) "noble; powerful; famous." Feminine of *Elmer*. Var., Almira, Elmina.

Eloise (Teutonic) "famous in battle." Var., Eloisa, Heloise, Louisa, Louise.

Elrica (Latin) "royal; ruler."

Elsa (Teutonic) "of nobility." Also means "dreamy; romantic" in French. Var. and dim., Else, Elsie, Elsy, Lisa, Lise.

Elva (Teutonic) "elfin; good." Var. and dim., Elfie, Ellie, Elvia, Elvie.

Elvina (Teutonic) "elve's friend." Feminine of *Elwin*. Var., Elvine.

Elvira (Latin) "fair; impartial." Also means "elfin" in Teutonic. Var. and dim., Elva, Elvera, Elvie, Elvire, Elwira.

Elysia (Greek) "heavenly happiness." Var. and dim., Elise, Elyse, Ilise, Ilysa, Ilyse.

Emeline (Teutonic) "industrious; intellectual." Var. and dim., Em, Emelin, Emelina, Emmeline, Emmy.

Emerald (Old French) "emerald; gem." Var. and dim., Em, Emerant, Emeroude, Emmie, Esmeralda.

Emily (Latin) "flatterer." Also means "industrious; artistic" in Teutonic. Feminine of *Emil*. Var. and dim., Aimil, Amalea, Amalia, Amalie, Amelia, Amélie, Ameline, Amelita, Amy, Eimile, Em, Emalia, Emelda, Emelia, Emelin, Emelina, Emeline, Emelita, Emelyne, Emera, Emilia, Emilie, Emiline, Emlyn, Emlynn, Emlynne, Emmaline, Emmalyn, Emmalynn, Emmalynne, Emmey, Emmi, Emmie, Emmy, Emmye, Millie, Milka.

Emina (Latin) "notable."

Emlyn (Teutonic) "industrious." Also means "adherent" in Welsh.

Emma (Teutonic) "nurse; ancestress; universal; energetic." Var. and dim., Em, Ema, Emelina, Emeline, Emelyne, Emie, Emmaline, Emmalyn, Emmalynn, Emmalynne, Emmeline, Emmi, Emmie, Emmy, Emmye.

Emogene (Greek) "well-loved child."

Ena (Gaelic) "fiery."

Engelberta (Teutonic) "shining angel."

Enid (Celtic) "pure; virtuous; woodlark."

Enrica (Teutonic) "head of house." Var., Enrika.

Erda (Teutonic) "earth." Var., Eartha, Erta, Herta, Hertha.

Erica (Teutonic) "ever mighty; eternally royal." Feminine of *Eric*. Var. and dim., Ericha, Erika, Rica, Ricki, Rickie, Ricky, Rika, Riki, Rikki.

Erin (Gaelic) "peaceable; tranquil." Var., Erina, Erinna.

Erline (Celtic) "a pledge." Also means "elfin" in Anglo-Saxon. Var., Arline, Erlina.

Erma (Latin) "royal; powerful." Also means "maiden of the army" in Teutonic. Var., Ermina, Erminia, Erminie, Hermia, Hermine, Herminia, Herminie, Hermione, Irma.

Erna (Celtic) "eagle; intent in purpose." Var., Ernaline.

Ernestine (Teutonic) "earnest; purposeful." Feminine of *Ernest*. Var. and dim., Erna, Ernaline, Ernesta, Teena, Tina.

Esme (Anglo-Saxon) "gracious protector." Var., Esma, Esmée.

Esmeralda (Greek) "emerald; jewel; bright hope." Var. and dim., Esme, Esmerelda.

Estelle (Latin) "a star." Var. and dim., Essie, Estel, Estele, Estell, Estella, Esther, Estrella, Estrellita, Stel, Stella, Stelle.

Esther (Hebrew) "a star; fortunate." Var. and dim., Easter, Eister, Essa, Essie, Essy, Esta, Ester, Esterel, Etti, Ettie, Etty, Hester, Hesther, Hettie, Hetty, Istar, Stella.

Estrella (Latin) "a star."

Ethel (Teutonic) "noble; ruler." Var., Ethelda, Ethelin, Ethelinda, Etheline, Ethelyn, Ethyl.

Ethelinda (Teutonic) "noble; wise; immortal." Var., Ethelin.

Etta (Teutonic) "small; home-ruler." Dim., Etty.

Eudocia (Greek) "esteemed; reputable." Var. and dim., Dorie, Doxie, Doxy, Eudosia, Eudoxia.

Eudora (Greek) "generous; joyous gift." Var. and dim., Dora, Eudore.

Eugenia (Greek) "of noble birth." Feminine of *Eugene*. Var. and dim., Eugénie, Gena, Gene, Genia, Genie, Gina.

Eulalia (Greek) "speaks beautifully. Var. and dim., Eula, Eulalie, Lallie.

Eunice (Greek) "joyfully victorious."

Euphemia (Greek) "well-spoken; reputable; accomplished." Var. and dim., Effie, Effy, Eppie, Eufemia, Euphémie, Phemie.

Eurydice (Greek) "wide space."

Eustacia (Greek) "peaceful; loyal; fertile." Var. and dim., Eustacie, Stacey, Stacia, Stacie, Stacy.

Evadne (Greek) "lucky; blossoming; water-nymph." Var., Euanthe.

Evangeline (Greek) "bringing pleasant news." Var. and dim., Eva, Evangelia, Eve, Vangie, Vangy.

Eve (Hebrew) "life." Var. and dim., Eba, Ebba, Eva, Evaleen, Eveleen, Evelina, Eveline, Evelyn, Evey, Evie, Evita, Evonne, Evvie, Evvy, Evy.

Evelyn (Celtic) "pleasant; light; life." Var. and dim., Aveline, Evalina, Evaline, Eveleen, Evelina, Eveline, Evvie, Lena, Lina.

F

Fabia (Latin) "grower of beans." Feminine of *Fabian*.

Faith (Latin) "faithful; trusting." Var. and dim., Fae, Fay, Faye, Fayth, Faythe.

Fanchon (Teutonic) "free." Dim., Fanchette.

Fancy (Greek) "fantasy." Var., Fancie.

Fanny (Teutonic) "free." Var. and dim., Fan, Fanni, Fannie.

Farica (Teutonic) "peaceable ruler." Var., Feriga.

Farrah (Middle English) "pleasing; lovely." Var. and dim., Farand, Farra, Farrand, Fayre.

Faustina (Latin) "lucky; fortunate." Var. and dim., Fausta, Faustena, Faustine.

Fawn (Latin) "young deer." Var., Faunia, Fawnia.

Fay (Old French) "fairy." Var. and dim., Fae, Faye, Fayette, Fayina.

Fayette (Old French) "little fairy."

Fedora (Greek) "heavenly gift." Feminine of *Theodore*. Var., Theodora.

Felice (Latin) "felicitous; joyous." Feminine of *Felix*. Var. and dim., Fee, Felicia, Felicidad, Félicie, Felicity, Felis, Félise, Felita, Feliza.

Fenella (Gaelic) "white-shouldered." Var., Finella.

Fern (Greek) "feather." Var., Ferne.

Fernanda (Teutonic) "life's adventuress." Feminine of *Ferdinand*. Var. and dim., Ferdinanda, Ferdinande, Fern, Fernand, Fernandina.

Fidelia (Latin) "faithful." Var. and dim., Fidela, Fidelity, Fidella.

Fifi (Hebrew) "she shall add." Var., Fifine.

Filma (Teutonic) "misty."

Fiona (Gaelic) "fair-complexioned." Var. and dim., Fio, Fionna, Phiona, Viona, Vionna.

Flavia (Latin) "golden-haired."

Fleta (Teutonic) "fleet; swift." Var., Fleda, Fleeta.

Flora (Latin) "flower." Var. and dim., Fiora, Fiore, Fleur, Fleurette, Flo, Flor, Flore, Florella, Floria, Florie, Floris, Florri, Florrie, Florry, Flossie.

Florence (Latin) "flowering; prosperous." Var. and dim., Fiorenza, Fleur, Fleurette, Flo, Flor, Flora, Florance, Flore, Florencia, Florentia, Florette, Flori, Floria, Florida, Florie, Florina, Florinda, Florine, Floris, Florri, Florrie, Florry, Floss, Flossi, Flossie, Flossy, Flower.

Florida (Latin) "blossoming; flowery."

Florina (Latin) "in bloom." Var., Florine.

Fonda (Latin) "profound; basic." Also means "fondness; tender" in Middle English.

Fortuna (Latin) "fortunate." Var., Fortune.

Frances (Latin) "free." Feminine of *Francis*. Var. and dim., Fan, Fanchette, Fanchon, Fancy, Fanechka, Fania, Fanni, Fannie, Fanny, Fanya, Fran, France, Francesca, Franci, Francie, Francine, Francisca, Franciska, Francoise, Francyne, Frank, Frankie, Franky, Franni, Frannie, Franny, Franziska.

Freda (Teutonic) "peace." Feminine of *Frederick*. Var. and dim., Frayda, Fredella, Fredie, Freida, Frida, Frieda.

Fredella (Teutonic) "peaceful elf."

Frederica (Teutonic) "peaceful ruler." Feminine of *Frederick*. Var. and dim., Farica, Federica, Fred, Freddi, Freddie, Freddy, Fredericka, Frédérique, Frerika, Friederike, Fritzi, Rica, Ricki, Rickie, Ricky, Rikki.

Freya (Old Norse) "noble." Var., Fraya.

Fulvia (Latin) "golden-haired."

G

Gabrielle (Hebrew) "of God's strength." Feminine of *Gabriel*. Var. and dim., Gabey, Gabi, Gabie, Gabriela, Gabriella, Gabrila, Gaby, Gavra.

Gail (Anglo-Saxon) "happy; vivacious." Var. and dim., Gael, Gale, Gayla, Gayle, Gayleen, Gaylene.

Galatea (Greek) "milky-white."

Gardenia (Latin) "white flower." Also means "from the garden" in Teutonic.

Garland (Latin) "chain of flowers."

Garnet (Latin) "garnet; red jewel." Var., Garnette.

Gay (Teutonic) "merry; light-hearted; lively." Var., Gae, Gaye.

Gazella (Latin) "gazelle; antelope."

Gelasia (Greek) "love of laughter."

Gemma (Latin) "gem; precious jewel."

Gene (Hebrew) "gracious gift of God." Var., Gena, Gina, Jean.

Geneva (Old French) "juniper tree." Var. and dim., Gena, Genevra, Janeva.

Genevieve (Teutonic) "white; fair; humble; white wave." Var. and dim., Gena, Geneva, Genevieve, Genevra, Gennie, Genny,

Genovera, Gina, Guinevere, Janeva, Jen, Jennie, Jenny.

Georgia (Greek) "tiller of the soil; farmer." Feminine of *George*. Var. and dim., George, Georgeanna, Georgeanne, Georgena, Georgetta, Georgette, Georgiana, Georgianna, Georgie, Georgienne, Georgina, Georgine, Giorgia.

Georgiana (Greek) "one who loves the earth; womanly dignity." Feminine of *George*. Var. and dim., Georgeanna, Georgeanne, Georgetta, Georgette, Georgi, Georgia, Georgianna, Georgianne, Georgie, Georgina, Georgine.

Geraldine (Teutonic) "mighty spear." Feminine of *Gerald*. Var. and dim., Deena, Dina, Geralda, Geraldina, Géraldine, Gerhardine, Geri, Gerri, Gerrie, Gerry, Giralda, Jeraldine, Jeralee, Jere, Jeri, Jerrie, Jerry.

Gerda (Teutonic) "protected." Var. and dim., Garda, Gerdi, Gerdie.

Germaine (Latin) "German." Var., Germain, Germana, Jermaine.

Gertrude (Teutonic) "all truth; strong spear." Var. and dim., Gert, Gerta, Gerti, Gertie, Gertrud, Gertruda, Gertrudis, Gerty, Trude, Trudi, Trudie, Trudy.

Gilberta (Teutonic) "shining promise." Feminine of *Gilbert*. Var. and dim., Berta, Berte, Berti, Bertie, Berty, Gigi, Gilberte, Gilbertina, Gilbertine, Gill, Gilli, Gillie, Gilly.

Gilda (Celtic) "handmaiden of God." Also means "gold-covered" in Anglo-Saxon. Var. and dim., Gilli, Golda.

Gillian (Latin) "downy-haired youth." Var. and dim., Jilana, Jill, Jillie, Jilly.

Gina (Latin) "queen."

Ginger (Latin) "ginger; spicy."

Giselle (Teutonic) "vow." Var., Gisela, Gisele, Gisella, Gizela.

Githa (Old Norse) "war." Var., Gytha.

Gladys (Latin) "lame; delicate; demure; capable; gladiolus." Feminine of *Claude*. Var. and dim., Glad, Gladdie, Gladi, Gladine, Gladis, Gladyce, Gleda.

Gleda (Anglo-Saxon) "gladness."

Glenna (Celtic) "from the glen." Feminine of *Glenn*. Var. and dim., Glen, Glenda, Glenine, Glenn, Glennie, Glennis, Glyn, Glynis, Glynnie, Glynnis.

Gloria (Latin) "glorious." Var. and dim., Glori, Gloriana, Gloriane, Glorianna, Glory.

Glynis (Gaelic) "from the glen." Var., Glynnis.

Godiva (Anglo-Saxon) "gift of God."

Golda (Teutonic) "golden-haired." Var. and dim., Goldarina, Goldia, Goldie, Goldina, Goldy, Goldye.

Grace (Latin) "graceful; attractive; full of gratitude; God's blessing." Var. and dim., Engracia, Gracia, Gracie, Gracye, Grata, Gratia, Gratiana, Gray, Grayce, Grazia.

Greer (Greek) "watchful." Feminine of *Gregory*.

Greta (Greek) "pearl." Var. and dim., Gredel, Gretchen, Grete, Gretel, Gretta.

Griselda (Teutonic) "stone battle-maid; heroine; meekly enduring." Var. and dim., Chriselda, Griseldis, Grishilda, Grishilde, Grissel, Grizel, Grizelda, Selda, Zelda.

Guinevere (Celtic) "white wave; fair-complexioned." Var. and dim., Fredi, Freddi, Freddie, Freddy, Gaynor, Gen, Genevieve, Genna, Genni, Gennie, Gennifer, Genny, Ginevra, Guenevere, Guenna, Guinna, Gwen, Gwenora, Gwenore, Janifer, Jen, Jenifer, Jennee, Jenni, Jennie, Jennifer, Jenny, Ona, Oona, Una, Vanora, Winifred, Winni, Winnie, Winny.

Gunhilda (Teutonic) "maid of war." Var., Gunhild.

Gustava (Scandinavian) "Gothic staff." Feminine of *Gustave*.

Gwen (Celtic) "white."

Gwendolyn (Celtic) "intellectual; understanding; white-browed." Var. and dim., Guendolen, Guenna, Gwen, Gwenda, Gwendolen, Gwendolin, Gwenn, Gwenni, Gwennie, Gwenny, Gwyn, Gwyneth, Gwynne, Wendi, Wendie, Wendy, Wynn.

Gwyneth (Celtic) "white; blessed." Var. and dim., Gweneth, Gwenith, Gwyn, Gwynedd, Gwynne, Winnie, Winny.

Gypsy (Old English) "wanderer." Var., Gipsy.

H

Hagar (Hebrew) "abandoned."

Haidee (Greek) "shy; virtuous; considerate."

Haldana (Old Norse) "half Danish."

Halfrida (Teutonic) "peaceful; noble."

Halimeda (Greek) "fond of the sea; seaweed." Dim., Hallie, Meda.

Hallie (Greek) "fascinated by the sea." Feminine of *Henry, Harold.* Var., Halimeda, Halli, Hally.

Hana (Japanese) "flower." Var., Hanae, Hanako.

Hannah (Hebrew) "full of grace; merciful; prayerful; good." Var. and dim., Anita, Ann, Anna, Anne, Annetta, Annette, Annice, Annie, Hana, Hanna, Hanni, Hannie, Hanny, Nan, Nana, Nancy, Nanette, Nanine, Nanny, Nanon, Nina, Ninetta, Ninon.

Happy (English) "joyful."

Haralda (Old Norse) "powerful in battle." Feminine of *Harold.* Var. and dim., Hallie, Hally, Harelda.

Harmony (Latin) "harmony; agreement." Var., Harmonia, Harmonie.

Harriet (Teutonic) "mistress of the home; head of the household." Feminine of *Henry*. Var. and dim., Harri, Harrie, Harrietta, Harriette, Harriot, Harrott, Hat, Hatti, Hattie, Hatty.

Hazel (Teutonic) "hazelnut tree; command." Var., Aveline.

Heather (Anglo-Saxon) "the flower, heather." Dim., Heath.

Hebe (Greek) "young." In Greek mythology, "goddess of youth and spring."

Hedda (Teutonic) "conflict; robe." Var. and dim., Heda, Heddi, Heddie, Heddy, Hedvige, Hedwig, Hedwiga, Hedy.

Hedwig (Teutonic) "struggle; strife." Var. and dim., Avice, Edvig, Heda, Hedda, Hedi, Hedvig, Hedvige, Hedwiga, Hedy.

Hedy (Greek) "pleasant; agreeable."

Heidi (German) "noble; kind."

Helen (Greek) "light." Probably the oldest feminine name in existence and the basis of many names quite different from itself. Var. and dim., Aila, Aileen, Ailene, Alaine, Aleen, Alyne, Eileen, Elaine, Elana, Elane, Elayne, Eleanor, Eleanora, Eleanore, Eleen, Elena, Elene, Eleni, Elenore, Eleanora, Eleonore, Elianora, Elinor, Elinore, Ella, Elladine, Elle, Ellen, Ellene, Ellette, Elli, Ellie, Elly, Ellyn, Ellynn, Elna, Elnora, Elnore, Elora, Elyn, Galina, Halina, Helaine, Helayne, Helena, Helene, Hélene, Helenka, Hellene, Helli, Ileana, Ileane, Ilene, Ilona, Ilonka, Jelena, Lana, Laine, Lainey, Lane, Layney, Leanor, Leena, Lena, Lenka, Lenni, Lennie, Lenora,

Lenore, Leonora, Leonore, Leora, Lina, Lora, Lorine, Nell, Nellette, Nelli, Nelliana, Nellie, Nelly, Nora, Norah, Valenka.

Helga (Teutonic) "holy."

Helma (Old German) "helmet; protection." Var., Hilma.

Heloise (Teutonic) "glorious warrior."

Henrietta (Teutonic) "ruler of the home; noble lady." Feminine of *Henry*. Var. and dim., Eiric, Enrichetta, Enriqueta, Etta, Etti, Ettie, Etty, Hallie, Harriet, Harriette, Harriott, Hatti, Hattie, Hatty, Hendrika, Henka, Henni, Hennie, Henrie, Henrieta, Henriette, Henrika, Henryetta, Hetti, Hettie, Hetty, Netta, Nettie, Netty, Yetta, Yettie, Yetty.

Hera (Greek) "queen." In Greek mythology, "the queen of the gods."

Hermia (Greek) "earthly; messenger."

Hermina (Latin) "godly." Var., Hermine, Ione.

Hermione (Greek) "of the earth." Feminine of *Herman*. Var. and dim., Erma, Hermia, Hermina, Hermine, Herminia, Ione.

Hermosa (Spanish) "beautiful."

Hertha (Greek) "mother earth." Var. and dim., Eartha, Erda, Erta, Ertha, Herta.

Hesper (Greek) "evening star."

Hester (Persian) "star; good fortune." Var. and dim., Esther, Hesper, Hestia, Hetti, Hettie, Hetty.

Hilary (Latin) "cheerful." Var., Hilaria, Hillarey, Hillary.

Hilda (Teutonic) "maiden of battle; strong; merciful." Var. and dim., Heidi, Hilde, Hildie, Hildy.

Hildegarde (Teutonic) "protective warrior-maid; stronghold." Var. and dim., Heidi, Hilda, Hildagard, Hildagarde, Hilde, Hildegard, Hildie, Hildy.

Hildreth (Teutonic) "counselor of war."

Hilma (Anglo-Saxon) "helmet." Var., Helma.

Holly (Anglo-Saxon) "the holly bush; good luck." Var., Hollie.

Honey (Old English) "sweet; beloved."

Honora (Latin) "honorable." Var. and dim., Honey, Honor, Honoria, Honorine, Nora, Norah, Noreen, Norine, Norri, Norrie, Norry.

Hope (Anglo-Saxon) "hope; optimism; desire; expectation; cheerful."

Horatia (Latin) "timekeeper." Feminine of *Horace*. Var., Horacia.

Hortense (Latin) "fragrant; sweet; gardener." Var., Hortensa, Hortensia, Ortensia.

Hoshi (Japanese) "starlike."

Huberta (Teutonic) "brilliant mind." Feminine of *Hubert*.

Huette (Teutonic) "small, bright-minded girl." Var., Huetta, Hugette, Hughette.

Hulda (Hebrew) "weasel." In Teutonic, "gracious; loved." In Norse, "muffled; covered." Var. and dim., Huldah, Huldie, Huldy.

Hyacinth (Greek) "hyacinth flower; purple." Var. and dim., Cinthie, Cynthie, Giacinta, Hyacintha, Hyacinthe, Hyacinthia, Hyacinthie, Jacenta, Jacinda, Jacinta, Jacintha, Jacinthe, Jackie, Jacky, Jacynth, Sinty.

Hypatia (Greek) "of superior intellect."

I

Ianthe (Greek) "violet; purple flower; delightful." Var. and dim., Ian, Iantha, Ianthina, Janthina.

Ida (Teutonic) "happy; industrious; youthful; prosperous." Var. and dim., Idalia, Idalina, Idaline, Idalla, Idelle, Idette.

Idalia (Greek) "happiness." Var., Idalina, Idaline.

Idele (Greek) "happy." Var., Idella.

Idona (Teutonic) "industrious worker." From the Norse goddess *Iduna*, who fed the gods apples to keep them youthful. Var., Idonea, Idonia, Iduna.

Ignatia (Latin) "ardent; fiery." Feminine of *Ignatius*. Var., Ignacia, Ignatzia.

Ileana (Greek) "from Ilium or Troy."

Ilka (Slavic) "industrious; vivacious; flattering." Var., Ilke, Ilonka, Milka.

Ilona (Hungarian) "beautiful." Var., Ilonka.

Ilsa (Hebrew) "oath of God." Var., Ilse.

Imogene (Latin) "image; likeness; pity for all who need." In Old English, "last born." Var., Emogene, Imogen, Imojean.

Ina (Greek) "pure."

Inez (Greek) "pure; chaste; gentle; humble." Var. and dim., Ina, Ines, Inesita, Ynes, Ynez.

Inga (Old Norse) "daughter; youthful battle chief." Var., Inge, Inger.

Ingrid (Old Norse) "daughter of a hero; beautiful." Var. and dim., Inga, Ingaberg, Inge, Ingeborg, Inger, Ingunna.

Iola (Greek) "dawn cloud; violet color." Var., Iole.

Iolanthe (Greek) "violet flower."

Ione (Greek) "precious violet-colored stone." Var., Iona, Ionia.

Irene (Greek) "peace; serenity." Var. and dim., Eirena, Eirene, Erena, Ira, Irena, Irina, Rena, Renata, Rene, Reni, Renie, Rennie, Renny, Rina.

Ireta (Greek) "angry; wrathful." Var., Iretta, Irette.

Iris (Greek) "the rainbow; the iris flower." Var., Irisa, Irita.

Irma (Latin) "powerful; noble." Var. and dim., Erma, Erme, Irme, Irmina, Irmine, Irminia, Irmy.

Irvette (Anglo-Saxon) "friend of the sea." Feminine of *Irving*.

Isa (Teutonic) "iron-willed; resolute."

Isabel (Hebrew) "consecrated to God." Var. and dim., Bel, Belia, Belicia, Belita, Bell, Bella, Belle, Ib, Ibbie, Ibby, Isa, Isabeau, Isabelita, Isabella, Isabelle, Isbel, Iseabal, Ishabel, Isobel, Issi, Issie, Issy, Izabel, Nib, Tibbie, Ysabel.

Isadora (Greek) "a gift." Either "gift of the moon" or "gift of *Isis*," Egyptian goddess of the moon, fertility, and motherhood. Feminine of *Isadore*. Var. and dim., Dora, Dori, Dory, Isidora, Issy, Izzy.

Isis (Egyptian) "supreme goddess, Egyptian goddess of the moon, fertility, and motherhood."

Isleen (Gaelic) "light; vision or dream."

Isolde (Celtic) "fair; lovely." Var., Iseult, Isolda, Isolt, Yseult.

Ita (Celtic) "thirsty for truth and knowledge."

Iva (Hebrew) "God's gracious gift." In Old French, "yew tree." Var., Ivah, Ivanna.

Ivana (Hebrew) "gracious gift of God." Feminine of *Ivan*. Var., Ivane.

Ivy (Hebrew) "ivy vine; clinging." Var., Iva.

J

Jacinda (Greek) "hyacinth flower; purple; beautiful." Var., Jacenta, Jacinta, Jacintha, Jacinthe, Jacynth.

Jacoba (Hebrew) "supplanter; substitute." Feminine of *Jacob*. Var. and dim., Jacki, Jackie, Jacky, Jacobina, Jacobine, Jakoba.

Jacqueline (Hebrew) "the supplanter." Feminine of *Jacob, James*. Var. and dim., Jackelyn, Jacki, Jackie, Jacklin, Jackquelin, Jackqueline, Jacky, Jaclin, Jaclyn, Jacquelyn, Jacquenetta, Jacquenette, Jacquetta, Jacquette, Jacqui, Jacquie, Jaqueline, Jaquenetta, Jaquenette, Jaquith.

Jade (Spanish) "jade; jewel."

Jane (Hebrew) "God's gracious gift." Feminine of *John*. Var. and dim., Gene, Gian, Gianina, Gianna, Giovanna, Jan, Jana, Janeczka, Janel, Janela, Janella, Janelle, Janet, Janeta, Janetta, Janette, Janey, Jania, Janice, Janie, Janina, Janine, Janis, Janith, Janka, Janna, Jannel, Jannelle, Janot, Jany, Janyte, Jasisa, Jayne, Jean, Jeanette, Jeaney, Jeanie, Jeanne, Jeannette, Jeannine, Jenda, Jenica, Jeniece, Jennet, Jennette, Jenni, Jennie, Jenny, Jess, Jessica, Jessie, Jinny, Jo Ann, Jo-Ann, Joan, Joana, Joanna, Joanne, Joeann, Johanna, Jone, Joni, Jonie, Juana, Juanita, Netta, Seonaid, Sheena, Shena, Sine, Sinead, Vania, Vanya, Zaneta.

Jasmine (Persian) "jasmine flower; fragrant blossom." Var. and dim., Jasmin, Jasmina, Jess, Jessamine, Jessamy, Jessamyn, Jessie, Yasmin.

Jay (Latin) "jaybird."

Jean (Hebrew) "gracious gift of God." Feminine of *John*. Var. and dim., Gene, Jeanette, Jeanie, Jeanne, Jeannette, Jeannine.

Jemima (Arabic) "dove; peace; purity." Also means "handsome" in Hebrew. Var. and dim., Jamima, Jem, Jemie, Jemimah, Jemmie, Jemmima, Jemmy, Mimi.

Jennifer (Celtic) "white-cheeked; fair." Var. and dim., Genna, Genni, Gennie, Gennifer, Genny, Jen, Jennee, Jenni, Jennie, Jenny.

Jessica (Hebrew) "wealthy; grace of God." Feminine of *Jesse*. Var. and dim., Jess, Jessalin, Jessalyn, Jessalynn, Jessie, Jessy.

Jewel (Latin) "precious gem; delight." Var., Jewell, Jewelle.

Jill (Greek) "youthful." Also means "girl; sweetheart" in Old English. Var. and dim., Jillana, Jilli, Jillie, Jilly.

Joan (Hebrew) "gracious gift of God." Feminine of *John*. Var. and dim., Joanna, Joanne, Jodi, Johanna, Jodie, Jody, Joni, Jonie, Juanita.

Jobina (Hebrew) "afflicted; persecuted; desire." Var. and dim., Jobey, Jobie, Joby, Jobye, Jobyna.

Jocelyn (Latin) "merry; just; fair." Var. and dim., Jocelin, Joceline, Jocelyne, Joseline, Joslyn, Josselyn, Joycelin, Justine, Lyn, Lynn.

Joletta (Latin) "the violet; modesty."

Josephine (Hebrew) "a reward; she shall add." Feminine of *Joseph*. Var. and dim., Fifi, Fifine, Fina, Giuseppina, Jo, Joette, Joey, Joline, Josefa, Josefina, Josepha, Josephe, Josephina, Josette, Josi, Josie, Josy, Pepita, Pheny.

Jovita (Latin) "joyful; merry."

Joy (Latin) "joy; delight." Var., Joya.

Joyce (Latin) "joyous." Var. and dim., Joice, Joy, Joyous.

Judith (Hebrew) "praised; admired." Var. and dim., Giuditta, Jodi, Jodie, Jody, Ju, Judi, Judie, Juditha, Judy, Judye.

Julia (Latin) "youthful; volatile, changeable." Feminine of *Julius*. Var. and dim., Gillie, Giuletta, Giulia, Jill, Joletta, Jule, Julee, Juli, Juliana, Juliane, Juliann, Julie, Julienne, Juliet, Julieta, Julietta, Juliette, Julina, Juline, Julita, Sile, Sileas.

June (Latin) "born in June; youthful." Var. and dim., Junetta, Junette, Junia, Juniata, Junie, Junieta, Junina, Junine, Junis.

Juno (Latin) "heavenly queen." In Roman mythology *Juno* was the goddess-queen of heaven.

Justine (Latin) "the just." Feminine of *Justin*. Var. and dim., Giustina, Justa, Justina, Justinn, Tina.

K

Kali (Sanskrit) "energetic."

Kalila (Arabic) "well-loved."

Kama (Sanskrit) "loved; desired; the Hindu god of love."

Kamaria (African) "like the moon."

Kameko (Japanese) "long-lived; turtle's child."

Kara (Greek) "pure." Also means "loved one" in Italian and "friend" in Gaelic. Var., Carina, Carine, Karena.

Karel (Latin) "strong; womanly." Feminine of *Charles, Carl.* Also means "joyful song" in Old French. Var., Karol, Karole, Karyl.

Karen (Greek) "pure; beautiful; intelligent." Var. and dim., Caren, Carin, Kara, Karena, Kareen, Kari, Karin, Karna, Karyn.

Karla (Teutonic) "strong." Feminine of *Charles.* Var. and dim., Karline, Karly.

Kate (Greek) "pure." Var. and dim., Katie, Katy.

Katherine (Greek) "pure; chaste." Var. and dim., Caitlin, Caitrin, Caren, Carin, Caron, Caryn, Cass, Cassie, Cassy, Catalina, Catarina, Cate, Caterina, Catha, Catharina, Catharine, Cathe, Cathee, Catherina, Catherine, Cathi, Cathie, Cathleen, Cathlene, Cathlin, Cathrine, Cathryn, Cathy, Cathyleen, Cati, Catie, Catlaina,

Catriona, Caty, Caye, Ekaterina, Ina, Kakalina, Kara, Karen, Karena, Kari, Karin, Karna, Karyn, Kasia, Kass, Kassi, Kassia, Kata, Katalin, Kate, Katerina, Katerine, Katey, Kath, Katha, Katharina, Katharine, Kathe, Katherin, Kathi, Kathie, Kathleen, Kathlene, Kathlina, Kathryn, Kathy, Kathye, Katie, Katina, Katinka, Katlyn, Katrina, Katrine, Katrinka, Katti, Katuscha, Katushka, Katya, Kay, Kaye, Ketti, Kettie, Ketty, Kit, Kitti, Kittie, Kitty, Trina, Trine, Trinette.

Kathleen (Greek) "pure little one." Var. and dim., Kate, Kath, Kathie, Kathlene, Katie, Katrine, Katrina, Kay, Kit, Kittie, Kitty.

Kay (Greek) "rejoicing." Var., Caye, Kaye.

Keely (Gaelic) "beautiful." Var., Keelia.

Keiko (Japanese) "revered."

Kelda (Old Norse) "bubbling spring." Var. and dim., Kela, Keldah, Kella, Kelly.

Kelly (Gaelic) "warrior maiden; brave." Var., Keli, Kelley, Kelli, Kellie.

Kendra (Anglo-Saxon) "one of knowledge; understanding." Var. and dim., Ken, Kendrath, Kendy.

Kerry (Gaelic) "dark one; dark-haired'"

Ketura (Hebrew) "incense; fragrance." Var., Keturah.

Keziah (Hebrew) "cassia plant."

Kim (Old English) "glorious ruler; noble."

Kimberly (Hebrew) "from the meadow of the royal fortress." Dim., Kim, Kimmie, Kimmy.

Kineta (Greek) "lively."

Kirby (Anglo-Saxon) "from the church town." Var., Kirbee, Kirbie.

Kirstin (Latin) "Christian." Var. and dim., Kirsten, Kirsti, Kirstie, Kirsty, Kristin, Kristina, Krysta.

Kora (Greek) "maiden." Var. and dim., Cora, Corabel, Corabella, Corabelle, Corella, Corena, Corene, Coretta, Corette, Corey, Cori, Corie, Corina, Corinna, Corinne, Coriss, Corissa, Correne, Corrie, Corrina, Corrine, Corry, Kore, Koren, Kori, Korie.

Koren (Greek) "lovely maiden." Var. and dim., Kore, Kori, Korie.

Kyla (Gaelic) "pretty; intelligent." Var. and dim., Kila, Kilah, Kyl, Kylah.

Kyna (Gaelic) "wise; intelligent." Feminine of *Conan*.

L

Lacey (Greek) "cheerful."

Lala (Slavic) "tulip."

Lalage (Greek) "talkative."

Lalita (Sanskrit) "pleasing; artless; straightforward."

Lana (Greek) "light." Var. and dim., Lanette, Lanna, Lanny.

Lanette (Anglo-Saxon) "a lane." Var., Lane.

Lani (Hawaiian) "sky."

Lara (Latin) "famous."

Laraine (Latin) "sea gull." Var., Larina, Larine.

Larissa (Greek) "cheerful." Dim., Lacey, Lissa.

Lark (Middle English) "skylark; singing."

Laura (Greek) "the laurel; victory; fame." Feminine of *Lawrence*. Var. and dim., Laraine, Lari, Laurè, Lauré, Laureen, Laurel, Lauren, Laurena, Laurene, Lauretta, Laurette, Laurey, Lauri, Laurice, Lolly, Lora, Loralie, Loree, Loreen, Lorelie, Loren, Lorena, Lorene, Lorenza, Loretta, Lorette, Lori, Lorie, Lorinda, Lorine, Lorita, Lorna, Lorne, Lorraine, Lorri, Lorrie, Lorry.

Laurel (Latin) "laurel; victory." Feminine of *Lawrence*. Var. and dim., Laurella, Laurie, Lori, Lorrie.

Lauren (Latin) "crown of laurel leaves; victory." Feminine of *Lawrence*. Var., Laureen, Laurena, Laurene.

Leveda (Latin) "purified." Var., Lavetta, Lavette.

Laverne (Old French) "springlike." Var. and dim., Laverna, La Verne, Vern, Verna, Verne.

Lavinia (Latin) "purified; lady from Rome." Var. and dim., Lavena, Lavina, Lavinie, Vin, Vina, Vinia, Vinni, Vinnie, Vinny.

Leah (Hebrew) "weary." Var. and dim., Lea, Leda, Lee, Leigh, Lia, Lida.

Leda (Greek) "lady." Var., Leta.

Lee (Anglo-Saxon) "meadow." Also means "poetic" in Gaelic. Var., Lea, Leann, Leeanna, Leigh.

Leila (Persian) "pearl." Also means "dark as night" in Arabic. Var. and dim., Layla, Lee, Leela, Leilah, Leilia, Lela, Lelah, Lelia, Lila.

Leilani (Hawaiian) "heavenly flower."

Lelia (Latin) "lily." Var., Lela, Lelah.

Lemuela (Hebrew) "dedicated to God." Feminine of *Lemuel*.

Lena (Greek) "light." Also means "temptress" in Latin. Var., Lenette, Lina.

Lenore (Greek) "light." Var. and dim., Lenora, Leonora, Leonore, Lora.

Leola (Greek) "lion."

Leoma (Anglo-Saxon) "light; brightness; radiance."

Leona (Latin) "lion." Feminine of *Leo*. Var. and dim., Lee, Lennie, Lenny, Leoine, Leola, Leone, Leonelle, Leoni, Leonia, Leonie, Léonie.

Leonarda (Teutonic) "brave as a lion." Feminine of *Leonard*. Var., Leonarde.

Leontine (Latin) "lionlike." Feminine of *Leo*. Var., Leontyne, Léontyne.

Leopoldine (Teutonic) "brave for the people; princess of the people." Feminine of *Leopold*. Var., Leopolda, Leopoldina.

Leota (Teutonic) "woman of the people." Var., Leoda.

Lesley (Celtic) "from the gray fort." Var. and dim., Les, Lesli, Leslie, Lesly, Lezlie.

Leta (Latin) "joy."

Letha (Greek) "forgetful." Var., Leda, Leitha, Leithia, Leta, Lethia.

Letitia (Latin) "joy; delight; gladness." Var. and dim., Laetitia, Leda, Léetice, Leta, Lethia, Leticia, Letisha, Letizia, Letti, Lettice, Lettie, Letty, Loutitia, Tish, Tisha.

Levina (Middle English) "lightning flash; fast."

Lexine (Greek) "helper of mankind."

Liana (Latin) "climbing vine; a bond." Var., Leana, Liane, Lianna, Lianne.

Libby (Hebrew) "dedicated to God." Var. and dim., Lib, Libbey, Libbie.

Lida (Slavic) "beloved of all." Var., Lyda.

Lilac (Persian) "lilac flower; blue color."

Lilis (Greek) "lily flower." Var., Lilias.

Lilith (Arabic) "of the night." Also means "serpent; evil; poor wife; in Hebrew. Var. and dim., Lil, Lilis, Lillis, Lillith, Lilly, Lily.

Lillian (Greek) "lily flower; purity." Var. and dim., Lela, Lelah, Lelia, Lil, Lila, Lilah, Lilas, Lili, Lilia, Lilian, Liliane, Lilias, Lilla, Lillah, Lilles, Lilli, Lillias, Lillie, Lilly, Lily, Lilyan, Lis, Liuka.

Lilybelle (Latin) "beautiful lily." Var. and dim., Lela, Lelah, Lelia, Lil, Lila, Lilah, Lilas, Lili, Lilia, Lilian, Liliana, Liliane, Lilias, Lilla, Lillah, Lilles, Lilli, Lillias, Lillibel, Lillie, Lilly, Lily, Lilyan, Lilybel, Lilybell.

Lina (Latin) "alluring." Var., Lena.

Linda (Latin) "beautiful." Var. and dim., Lind, Lindi, Lindie, Lindy, Lynd, Lynda.

Lindsey (Old English) "from the island of pools and linden trees." Feminine of *Lindsay*.

Linette (Celtic) "graceful." Also means "the linnet gird" in Anglo-Saxon and "little lioness" in Old French. Var. and dim., Lanette, Linet, Linn, Linnet, Linnetta, Linnette, Lynette, Lynn, Lynnet, Lynnette, Netta.

Linnea (Old Norse) "lime tree." Var., Lynnea.

Lisa (Hebrew) "oath of God; Mona Lisa." Var. and dim., Leesa, Lise, Lisetta, Lisette, Liza, Lizzie, Lissy.

Lisbeth (Hebrew) "consecrated to God." Var. and dim., Lisabet, Lisabetta, Lisabette, Lizabeth.

Livia (Latin) "the olive." Var. and dim., Liv, Livvie.

Lodema (Anglo-Saxon) "guide."

Lois (Greek) "battle maiden; brave; a beautiful vision." Feminine of *Lewis*.

Lola (Latin) "sadness; grief." Also means "strong" in Teutonic. Feminine of *Charles*. Var., Loleta, Lolette, Lolita, Lulita.

Lona (Middle English) "alone; solitary."

Lora (Latin) "the laurel; victory." Var., Laura, Lorella, Lorelle, Lori, Lorita.

Lorelei (Teutonic) "a siren; alluring." Var. and dim., Lorilee, Lura, Lurette, Lurine, Lurleen, Lurlene, Lurlina.

Lorena (Latin) "the laurel; victory." Feminine of *Lawrence*. Var., Lorna.

Lorraine (Teutonic) "famous warrior." Var. and dim., Laraine, Lorain, Loraine, Lori, Lorrayne.

Lotus (Greek) "lotus flower; forgetfulness."

Louise (Teutonic) "famous battle maiden; a beautiful vision." Feminine of *Lewis*. Var. and dim., Alison, Allison, Aloisa, Aloise, Aloisia, Aloysia, Eloisa, Eloise, Héloïse, Lisette, Lois, Loise, Lola, Lolita, Lou, Louisa, Louisette, Loyce, Lu, Ludovika, Ludwiga, Luisa, Luise, Lulie, Lulita, Lulu.

Love (Old English) "love; strong, tender affection."

Luana (Teutonic) "graceful maiden of battle." Var. and dim., Lewanna, Lou, Louanna, Louanne, Lu, Luane, Luann, Luwana.

Lucille (Latin) "light." Var. and dim., Lucilla, Lucy.

Lucinda (Latin) "light." Dim., Cindy, Lucky.

Lucretia (Latin) "bringer of light; gain; riches; reward." Var. and dim., Lucrèce, Lucrecia, Lucrezia, Lucy.

Lucy (Latin) "light; bringer of light; born at daybreak." Feminine of *Lucius*. Var. and dim., Lu, Luce, Lucette, Lucia, Luciana, Lucida, Lucie, Lucienne, Lucile, Lucilla, Lucille, Lucina, Lucinda, Lucine, Lucita, Lulu, Luz.

Ludella (Teutonic) "people." Also means "famous elf; pixie" in Old English.

Ludmilla (Teutonic) "people." Also means modest." Var. and dim., Ludie, Ludmila, Ludovika.

Luella (Latin) "making atonement; the appeaser." Also means "famous elf" in Old English. Var. and dim., Ella, Loella, Lou, Louella, Lu, Luelle, Lula, Lulu.

Luna (Latin) "moon; shining."

Lunetta (Italian) "little moon." Dim., Luna, Lunna.

Lupe (Latin) "wolf."

Lurline (Teutonic) "alluring." Var. and dim., Lura, Lurette, Lurleen, Lurlene.

Luvena (Teutonic) "little loved one."

Lydia (Greek) "woman from Lydia; cultured." Var. and dim., Liddy, Lidia, Lydie.

Lynn (Anglo-Saxon) "a cascade; waterfall." Var. and dim., Linn, Lyn, Lynna, Lynne, Lynelle, Lynette.

Lyris (Greek) "the lyre or harp; musical." Var., Liris, Lyra.

Lysandra (Greek) "liberator of mankind." Dim., Sandra.

M

Mab (Celtic) "mirth; joy." Var., Mave, Mavis, Meave.

Mabel (Latin) "lovable; amiable." Var. and dim., Amabel, Belle, Mab, Mabelle, Mable, Mae, Maible, Maybelle.

Madeline (Hebrew) "woman of Magdala; magnificent; tower of strength." Var. and dim., Dalenna, Lena, Lenna, Lina, Linn, Lynn, Lynne, Mada, Madalena, Madalyn, Maddalena, Maddi, Maddie, Maddy, Madel, Madelaine, Madeleine, Madelena, Madelene, Madelina, Madella, Madelle, Madelon, Madge, Madid, Madlen, Madlin, Mady, Magda, Magdala, Magdalen, Magdalcna, Magdalene, Magdaline, Maidel, Maighdlin, Mala, Malena, Malina, Marleah, Marleen, Marlena, Marlene, Marline, Matty, Maud, Maude.

Madge (Greek) "a pearl."

Madra (Latin) "mother."

Magnolia (Anglo-Saxon) "flower of the magnolia tree." Dim., Mag, Maggie, Nola, Nolie.

Mahala (Hebrew) "tenderness." Var. and dim., Mahalah, Mahalia, Mahla, Mehala.

Maia (Greek) "motherly; nurse." Var., Maya.

Maida (Anglo-Saxon) "maiden." Var. and dim., Maddie, Maddy, Mady, Magd, Magda, Maidel, Maidena, Maidene, Maidie, Maidy, Mayda, Mayde, Maydena.

Maisie (Greek) "a pearl."

Majesta (Latin) "majestic."

Malca (Teutonic) "active; industrious." Var., Malcah.

Malina (Hebrew) "a tower; magnificent."

Malinda (Greek) "sweet; gentle." Var. and dim., Lindy, Malena, Malina, Malinde, Mallie, Mally, Melina.

Malva (Greek) "soft." Var., Melba, Melva.

Malvina (Gaelic) "heroic." Feminine of *Malvin*. Var. and dim., Mal, Malva, Malvie, Mel, Melva, Melvie, Melvine.

Manuela (Spanish) "God is with us." Feminine of *Emanuel*. Var. and dim., Ela, Emanuela, Manella, Mannuela.

Mara (Hebrew) "bitter." Var., Marah, Maralina, Maraline, Mari.

Marcella (Latin) "belonging to Mars; martial." Feminine of *Marc*. Var. and dim., Marcela, Marcelle, Marcellina, Marcelline, Marcie, Marcile, Marcille, Marcy, Marquita.

Marcia (Latin) "of Mars; warrior." Feminine of *Marc*. Var. and dim., Marcelia, Marcella, Marchita, Marcie, Marcile, Marcille, Marcy, Marquita, Marsha, Martia.

Marelda (Teutonic) "famous maiden of battle." Var., Mareld, Marilda, Marolda.

Marella (Teutonic) "little Mary." Var., Marela, Marelya, Maria.

Margaret (Greek) "a pearl." Var. and dim., Daisy, Gredel, Greta, Gretal, Gretchen, Grete, Gretel, Grethal, Grethel, Gretta, Madge, Mag, Maggi, Maggie, Maggy, Maiga, Maisie, Marga, Margalo, Margareta, Margarete, Margaretha, Margarethe, Margaretta, Margarette, Margarita, Marge, Margery, Marget, Margette, Margherita, Margi, Margie, Margit, Margo, Margot, Marguerita, Marguerite, Margy, Marje, Marji, Marjie, Marjorie, Marjory, Marjy, Marketa, Meg, Megan, Meggi, Meggie, Meggy, Meghan, Meta, Midge, Moggy, Peg, Pegeen, Peggi, Peggie, Peggy, Rita.

Marian (English) "graceful." Var., Mariam, Mariana, Marianna, Marianne, Marion, Maryann, Maryanne.

Maribel (Hebrew-Latin) "the beautiful Mary." Var., Maribelle, Marybelle.

Marigold (Anglo-Saxon) "like the golden marigold flower." Var., Marigolde.

Marina (Latin) "of the sea." Var. and dim., Marna, Marne, Marni, Marnie, Marinita, Rena, Rina.

Maris (Latin) "sea star." Var. and dim., Mari, Marisa, Marissa, Marras, Marris, Marys, Meris.

Marjorie (Greek) "a pearl." Var. and dim., Mag, Maggie, Marge, Margery, Margie, Margo, Margory, Margy, Marje, Marjie, Marjory, Marjy.

Marlene (Hebrew) "elevated." Var. and dim., Marla, Marleen, Marleene, Marlena, Marline, Marlyn, Marna.

Marmara (Greek) "radiant; charming; magnetic."

Martha (Aramaic) "a lady; ruler of the home." Var. and dim., Mart, Marta, Martella, Martelle, Marth, Marthe, Marthena, Marti, Martie, Martina, Martita, Marty, Martynne, Matti, Mattie, Matty, Pat, Patsy, Patti, Pattie, Patty.

Martina (Latin) "warlike; martial." Feminine of *Martin*. Var. and dim., Marta, Marteena, Marti, Martie, Martine, Marty, Teena, Tina.

Marvel (Latin) "wonderful; a miracle." Var. and dim., Marva, Marvela, Marvella, Marvelle.

Mary (Hebrew) "bitter." Var. and dim., Mae, Mair, Maire, Mairi, Malia, Mall, Mame, Mamie, Manette, Manon, Manya, Mara, Marabel, Maraline, Marea, Maren, Marella, Maretta, Mari, Maria, Mariam, Marian, Marianna, Marianne, Marice, Maridel, Marie, Mariel, Marietta, Mariette, Marilee, Marilin, Marilla, Marilyn, Marin, Marion, Mariquilla, Maris, Marisa, Mariska, Marissa, Marita, Maritsa, Marja, Marje, Marla, Marlo, Marnia, Marquita, Marris, Marya, Maryann, Maryanne, Marylin, Marysa, Maryse, Masha, Maura, Maure, Maureen, Maurene, Maurine, Maurise, Maurita, Maurizia, Mavra, May, Mayme, Mearr, Meridel, Meriel, Meris, Merrili, Mia, Mimi, Minette, Minnie, Minny, Miriam, Mitzi, Mitzie, Moira, Moll, Mollie, Molly, Morene, Moya, Muire, Murial, Muriel, Murielle, Poll, Polly.

Matilda (Teutonic) "mighty in battle." Var. and dim., Maitilde, Mat, Matelda, Mathilda, Mathilde, Matilde, Matti, Mattie, Matty, Maud, Maude, Tilda, Tillie, Tilly.

Mattea (Hebrew) "gift of God." Feminine of *Matthew*. Var., Mathea, Mathia, Matthea, Matthia.

Maude (Teutonic) "brave in battle." Var. and dim., Maud, Maudie.

Maureen (Gaelic) "little Mary." Also means "dark-complexioned" in Old French. Feminine of *Maurice*. Var, and dim., Maura, Maurene, Maurine, Maurise, Maurita, Maurizia, Moira, Mora, Moreen, Morena, Moria.

Mavis (Celtic) "the song-thrush."

Maxine (Latin) "the greatest; superior." Feminine of *Maximilian*. Var. and dim., Max, Maxi, Maxie, Maxime, Maxy.

May (Latin) "born in May; great one." Also means "kinswoman" in Anglo-Saxon and "maiden" in Middle English. Var., Mae, Maia, Maya, Maye.

Meara (Gaelic) "mirth."

Medea (Greek) "ruler; cnchantress." Also means "middle child" in Latin. Var., Madora, Meda, Media, Medora.

Megan (Greek) "strong; great." Var. and dim., Meg, Meggi, Meggie, Meggy, Meghan.

Mehitabel (Hebrew) "favored by God." Var. and dim., Hetty, Hitty, Mehetabel, Mehitabelle, Mehitable, Metabel.

Melanie (Greek) "darkness; dressed in black; Var. and dim., Malan, Mel, Mela, Melan, Melania, Melany, Melli, Mellie, Melina, Melloney, Melly, Milena.

Melantha (Greek) "dark flower."

Melba (Greek) "soft; slender; Also means "mallow flower" in Latin and "handmaiden" in Celtic. Var., Malva, Melbia, Melva.

Melina (Greek) "gentle." Also means "the color of the yellow canary" in Latin. Var., Melana.

Melinda (Greek) "soft; kind." Var. and dim., Linda, Lindy, Lynda, Malina, Malinda, Malinde, Mandy, Melinde.

Melissa (Greek) "honey; bee." Var. and dim., Lisa, Lissa, Malissa, Mel, Melesa, Melessa, Melicent, Melisa, Melisande, Melise, Melisenda, Melisent, Melisse, Melissent, Melita, Melitta, Melli, Mellicent, Mellie, Melly, Melosa, Milicent, Millicent, Millie, Millisent, Milly, Misha, Missie, Missy.

Melody (Greek) "song." Var. and dim., Lodie, Mel, Melodie.

Mercedes (Spanish) "merciful." Dim., Merci, Mercy.

Mercie (Anglo-Saxon) "from Mercia."

Mercy (French-Latin) "merciful; compassionate." Var., Mercedes.

Meredith (Old Welsh) "magnificent." Also means "guardian from the sea" in Celtic. Var. and dim., Meridth, Merridie, Merry.

Merle (Latin) "a blackbird." Var. and dim., Meria, Merl, Merla, Merlina, Merline, Merola, Meryl, Myrie, Myrlene.

Merritt (Anglo-Saxon) "of merit." Var. and dim., Merit, Merri, Merry.

Merry (Anglo-Saxon) "merry; pleasant; happy; mirthful." Var. and dim., Marrilee, Meri, Merie, Merrie, Merrielle, Merrilee, Merrili.

Meta (Latin) "ambitious." Var. and dim., Eta, Meda, Mettah.

Mia (Latin) "mine; belonging to me."

Michelle (Hebrew) "who is like God?" Feminine of *Michael*. Var. and dim., Mia, Micaela, Michaela, Michaele, Michaelina, Michaeline, Michaella, Michel, Michelina, Micheline, Michella, Mickey, Micki, Mickie, Micky, Midge, Miguela, Miguelita, Mikaela, Miquela.

Mignon (Old French) "dainty; delicate; darling." Var. and dim., Mignonette, Mignonne, Mignonnette.

Mildred (Teutonic) "gentle counselor; mild power." Var. and dim., Mil, Mildrid, Milli, Millie, Milly.

Millicent (Teutonic) "industrious; strong." Var. and dim., Lissa, Mel, Melicent, Melisande, Melisenda, Mellicent, Mellie,

Mellisent, Melly, Mil, Milicent, Milissent, Milli, Millie, Millisent, Milly, Milzie, Missie, Missy.

Minerva (Greek) "wisdom." Dim., Min, Minette, Minnie, Minny.

Minna (Teutonic) "love; remembrance." Var. and dim., Min, Mina, Minda, Mindy, Minetta, Minette, Mini, Minne, Minnette, Minnie, Minny.

Mira (Latin) "wonderful." Var., Mireille, Mirella, Mirelle, Mirilla, Myra, Myrilla.

Mirabel (Latin) "very beautiful; wondrous." Var. and dim., Bell, Belle, Mira, Mirabella, Mirabelle.

Miranda (Latin) "admirable." Dim., Mira, Myra, Randie, Randy.

Miriam (Hebrew) "bitter; rebellious." Dim., Mimi, Minnie, Mitzi.

Modesty (Latin) "modest; humble." Var. and dim., Desta, Deste, Modesta, Modeste, Modestia, Modestine.

Moira (Greek) "meritable." Also means "soft" in Celtic and "great" in Gaelic. Var. and dim., Moina, Moir, Moya, Moyna, Moyra, Oira.

Mona (Greek) "alone; unique." Also means "great; noble" in Celtic. Var., Moina, Moyna.

Monica (Greek) "wisdom; victory." Also means "advisor" in Latin. Var. and dim., Mona, Monca, Monique.

Morgana (Old Welsh) "from the seashore." Feminine of *Morgan*. Var., Morgan.

Morna (Gaelic) "gentle; loved."

Moselle (Hebrew) "saved from the water." Feminine of *Moses*. Var., Mozelle.

Muriel (Arabic) "myrrh; bitter.: Also means "sea-bright" in Gaelic. Var. and dim., Merial, Meriel, Mur, Murial, Murielle.

Musetta (Old French) "a quiet, tender song." Var., Musette.

Myra (Greek) "abundant." Also means "wonderful" in Latin. Var., Mira, Mirilla, Myrilla.

Myrna (Gaelic) "gentle; polite." Var., Merna, Mirna, Moina, Morna, Moyna.

Myrtle (Greek) "myrtle; crown of victory." Var. and dim., Merta, Mertice, Mertle, Mirtle, Myrt, Myrta, Myrtia, Myrtice, Myrtie, Myrtilla, Myrtis.

N

Nadine (Slavic) "hope." Var. and dim., Nada, Nadia, Nadiya, Nady, Nadya, Natka.

Naida (Latin) "water nymph."

Nancy (Hebrew) "grace." Var. and dim., Nan, Nana, Nance, Nancee, Nancey, Nanci, Nancie, Nanelle, Nanelia, Nanetta, Nanette, Nanice, Nanine, Nanna, Nannie, Nanny, Nanon, Netti, Nettie, Netty, Ninon.

Naomi (Hebrew) "pleasant; sweet." Var. and dim., Naoma, Noami, Noemi, Nomi.

Nara (Celtic) "happy."

Narda (Persian) "the anointed; fragrant; joyful." Var., Nara.

Nata (Sanskrit) "dancer."

Natalie (Latin) "natal or birth day; Christmas child." Var. and dim., Nat, Nata, Natala, Natale, Natalee, Natalia, Natalina, Nataline, Natascha, Natasha, Nathalia, Nathalie, Natica, Natika, Natividad, Nattie, Natty, Netta, Netti, Nettie, Netty, Noel, Noelle, Novella.

Nathania (Hebrew) "gift of God." Feminine of *Nathan*. Var., Nathene.

Neala (Gaelic) "champion." Feminine of *Neal*. Var. and dim., Neal, Neela, Neila.

Neda (Slavic) "Sunday's child." Also means "wealthy guardian" in Anglo-Saxon. Feminine of *Edward*. Var. and dim., Ned, Nedda, Neddy, Nedi.

Nelda (Old English) "of the elder tree."

Nerine (Greek) "nymph of the sea; swimmer." Var. and dim., Nereen, Nerice, Nerin, Nerina, Nerissa.

Nerissa (Greek) "of the sea." Var., Nerita.

Nevada (Latin) "snowy." Var. and dim., Nava, Navada, Neva, Vada.

Nicole (Greek) "victory of the people." Feminine of *Nicholas*. Var. and dim., Colette, Cosetta, Cosette, Nichola, Nicki, Nickie, Nicky, Nicola, Nicoletta, Nicolette, Nicoli, Nicolina, Nicoline, Niki, Nikki, Nikola.

Nike (Greek) "victory." Var., Nika.

Nila (Latin) "the river Nile."

Nina (Spanish) "well-loved daughter." Var. and dim., Nina, Ninetta, Ninette, Ninon.

Nissa (Scandinavian) "friendly elf or brownie." Var. and dim., Nisse, Nissie, Nissy.

Nita (Latin) "neat." Also means "a bear" in Choctaw Indian. Var., Netta.

Noel (Latin) "Christmas; Christmas child." Feminine of *Noel*. Var. and dim., Noel, Noella, Noelle, Noellyn, Noelyn, Novelia.

Nola (Latin) "small bell." Also means "famous; noble" in Celtic. Var., Nolana.

Noleta (Latin) "unwilling."

Nolita (Latin) "the olive." Feminine of *Oliver*. Var. and dim., Lita, Noli, Nolitta.

Nona (Latin) "ninth-born." Var. and dim., Nonette, Nonie, Nonna.

Nora (Latin) "honor." Var. and dim., Norah, Norrie.

Norberta (Teutonic) "bright heroine." Also means "Njord's brilliance" in Old Norse.

Norma (Latin) "model; pattern." Var. and dim., Noreen, Normi, Normi, Normie.

Novia (Latin) "new." Var., Nova, Novah.

Nunciata (Latin) "bringer of news."

Nydia (Latin) "a refuge." Var., Nidia.

Nyssa (Greek) "beginning point." Also means "reaching for a goal" in Latin.

O

Obelia (Greek) "a pillar."

Octavia (Latin) "eighth-born." Feminine of *Octavius.* Var. and dim., Octave, Octavie, Ottavia, Tave, Tavi, Tavia, Tavie, Tavy.

Odele (Greek) "a melody."Var. and dim., Odel, Odelet, Odelette, Odell.

Odelia (Teutonic) "wealthy; rich." Feminine of *Odell.* Var. and dim., Odelinda, Odella, Odetta, Odette, Odila, Odile, Odilia, Otha, Othelia, Othilia, Ottilie, Uta.

Odessa (Greek) "voyager."

Odette (Old French) "homemaker; patriotic." Var. and dim., Odelia, Odet, Odetta.

Ola (Old Norse) "resembling an ancestor." Feminine of *Olaf.*

Olga (Teutonic) "sacred." Var. and dim., Elga, Helga, Olenka, Olia, Olive, Olivia, Olva.

Olinda (Latin) "sweet-smelling."

Olive (Latin) "the olive." Feminine of *Oliver.* Var. and dim., Liva, Livi, Livia, Livvi, Livvie, Livvy, Livy, Nola, Nolana, Nolita, Noll, Nollie, Olga, Olia, Olivette, Olivia, Olli, Ollie, Olly, Olva.

Olympia (Greek) "heavenly; from Olympus" Var. and dim., Olimpia, Olympe, Olympias, Olympie, Pia.

Oma (Arabic) "ruler." Feminine of *Omar.*

Ona (Latin) "oneness." Var., Oona.

Ondine (Latin) "a wave." Var., Undine.

Opal (Sanskrit) "the opal; precious stone."

Ophelia (Greek) "wise; immortal." Var. and dim., Ofelia, Ofilia, Ophélie, Phelia.

Oralie (Latin) "golden; seashore." Also means "money" in Anglo-Saxon. Var. and dim., Ora, Orabel, Orabelle, Oralia, Orel, Oriel, Orielda, Oriole, Orlena, Orlene, Orlina.

Orea (Latin) "from the mountain."

Oriana (Latin) "golden one; dawn." Var., Oriane.

Orna (Latin) "decorative." Also means "olive-colored" in Gaelic. Var. and dim., Ornas, Ornie.

Orpah (Hebrew) "young deer."

Orva (Anglo-Saxon) "friend in combat." Also means "valued as gold" in Old French. Feminine of *Orvin*. Var. and dim., Oru, Orvah, Orvan.

P

Page (Anglo-Saxon) "knight's attendant."

Paige (Anglo-Saxon) "child; youthful." Var., Page.

Pallas (Greek) "wisdom; knowledge." Dim., Palla.

Palma (Latin) "a palm tree; born on Palm Sunday." Var., Palmira, Palmyra.

Pamela (Greek) "all-honey; sweet; loving; kind." Var. and dim., Pam, Pamelina, Pamella, Pammi, Pammie, Pammy

Pandora (Greek) "all-gifted; many-talented." Dim., Dorie.

Panphila (Greek) "all-loving." Var., Panfila.

Pansy (Greek) "the pansy flower; fragrant." Also means "a thought" in French. Var., Pansie.

Panthea (Greek) "of all the Gods." Var. and dim., Panta, Panthia, Thea, Thia.

Parthenia (Greek) "maidenly; virginal."

Patience (Latin) "patient; enduring fortitude." Dim., Pate.

Patricia (Latin) "patrician; of nobility; wellborn." Feminine of *Patrick*. Var. and dim., Pat, Patricia, Patrice, Patrizia, Patsy, Patti, Pattie, Patty, Tricia, Trish.

Paula (Latin) "little." Feminine of *Paul*. Var. and dim., Paola, Paolina, Paule, Pauletta,

Paulette, Pauli, Paulie, Paulina, Pauline, Paulin, Paulita, Pauly, Pavia, Pol, Polly.

Peace (Latin) "peaceful; tranquil."

Pearl (Latin) "a pearl; precious gem." Var. and dim., Pearla, Pearle, Pearline, Perl, Perla, Perle, Perlie, Perline, Perry.

Peggy (Greek) "a pearl." Var. and dim., Peg, Pegeen, Pegene, Peggoty.

Pelagia (Greek) "of the sea." Var., Pelagie.

Penelope (Greek) "weaver." Var. and dim., Pen, Penelopa, Pennie, Penny.

Penthea (Greek) "fifth-born." Var. and dim., Pentha, Pentheam, Pentheas.

Peony (Greek) "the peony flower; healer." Var., Peonie.

Pepita (Spanish) "she shall add." Var. and dim., Pepi, Peta.

Perdita (Latin) "lost."

Perfecta (Latin) "perfect."

Pernella (Old French) "small rock." Also means "young woman" in Celtic. Feminine of *Peter*. Var., Parnella, Pernelle.

Persis (Greek) "woman from Persia." Var., Persas.

Petra (Greek) "rock; stone." Feminine of *Peter*. Var. and dim., Pet, Peta, Pete, Peti, Petie, Petrina, Petronella, Petronia, Petronilla, Petronille, Pier, Pierette, Pierrette, Perrine, Petta.

Petula (Latin) "peevish; seeking." Var. and dim., Pet, Petulah, Petulia.

Petunia (American Indian) "the petunia flower; reddish-purple."

Phedra (Greek) "bright." Var., Phaedra, Phaidra.

Phenice (Hebrew) "from the palm tree." Var. and dim., Pheni, Phenica, Phenicia, Venice.

Philana (Greek) "lover of all God created; loved by all." Var. and dim., Phil, Phila, Philana, Philene, Philida, Philina, Philine, Phillane, Phillina.

Philantha (Greek) "flower-lover."

Philberta (Teutonic) "exceptionally brilliant."

Philippa (Greek) "lover of horses." Feminine of *Philip*. Var. and dim., Felipa, Filippa, Phil, Philipa, Philippe, Philippine, Phillie, Philly, Pippa, Pippy.

Philomena (Greek) "the nightingale; lover of the moon." Var. and dim., Phil, Philomel.

Philona (Greek) "lover of mankind." Var. and dim., Filomena, Mena, Phil.

Phoebe (Greek) "shining; bright; wise." Var., Phebe.

Phyllis (Greek) "a green bough." Var. and dim., Filide, Philis, Phillis, Phyl, Phylis, Phyllida, Phyllys.

Pia (Italian) "devout; pious."

Pierrette (French) "steady." Feminine of *Peter*.

Pilar (Spanish) "a pillar; foundation."

Piper (Old English) "pipe-player."

Placida (Latin) "serene; calm." Var., Placidia.

Pomona (Latin) "fruitful."

Poppy (Latin) "the poppy flower; fragrant."

Portia (Latin) "pig; an offering." Var., Porcia.

Prima (Latin) "first-born." Var., Primalia.

Primavera (Latin) "springtime."

Primrose (Latin) "the first rose." Dim., Rose, Rosie.

Priscilla (Latin) "from ancient times; of long lineage." Var. and dim., Pris, Prisca, Priscella, Prisilla, Prissie, Prissy, Sil.

Prudence (Latin) "prudent; cautious; intelligent; having foresight." Var. and dim., Pru, Prud, Prudi, Prudie, Prudy, Prue.

Prunella (Old French) "prune- or plum-colored; purple."

Psyche (Greek) "the soul."

Q

Quartas (Latin) "fourth-born."

Quenby (Scandinavian) "a wife; womanly."

Quenna (Teutonic) "a woman; wife." Also means "a queen" in Old English. Var. and dim., Queenie, Queeny, Quenie.

Querdia (Spanish) "loved one." Dim., Erida, Queri, Rida.

Quinta (Latin) "fifth-born." Feminine of *Quentin*. Var., Quintilla, Quintina.

R

Rachel (Hebrew) "a ewe; little lamb; gentle; innocent; naive." Var. and dim., Rachael, Rachele, Rachelle, Rae, Rahel, Rakel, Raquel, Raquela, Ray, Rey, Rochell, Rochelle, Shell, Shelley, Shellie, Shelly.

Radella (Old English) "counselor." Var., Radilla.

Rae (Old English) "a doe; female deer." Var., Ray, Raya.

Raina (Teutonic) "might; power." Also means "queen" in French-Latin. Var., Rainah, Rayna, Raynata, Regina.

Ramona (Teutonic) "protector; wise; mighty." Feminine of *Raymond*. Var. and dim., Mona, Rama, Ramonda, Romona.

Rana (Sanskrit) "royal." Var., Ranee, Rani, Rania, Ranice.

Randy (Latin) "admired." Also means "shield" in Anglo-Saxon. Feminine of *Randolf*. Var., Randie.

Raphaela (Hebrew) "blessed healer; healed by God." Feminine of *Raphael*. Var., Rafaela, Raffaelle.

Rebba (Hebrew) "fourth-born." Var. and dim., Reba, Rebah.

Rebecca (Hebrew) "bound; captivator; enchantingly beautiful." Var. and dim., Becca, Becka, Becki, Beckie, Becky, Bekki, Reba, Rebeca, Rébecca, Rebeka, Rebekah,

Rebekka, Ree, Reeba, Riba, Riva, Rivalee, Rivi, Rivkah, Rivy.

Regina (Latin) "queen; queenly." Var. and dim., Gina, Gine, Queenie, Ragina, Raina, Regan, Reggi, Reggie, Regine, Reina, Reine, Reyna, Rina.

Rena (Hebrew) "song."

Renata (Latin) "reborn." Var. and dim., Renae, Renate, Rene, Renee, Renée, Renie, Rennie.

Rene (Greek) "peace." Dim., Renie.

Renita (Latin) "self-poised." Var. and dim., Nita, Rani, Reneta, Riti.

Reseda (Latin) "the mignonette flower."

Reva (Latin) "to regain strength."

Rexana (Latin) "regal grace." Var., Rexanna, Rexanne.

Rhea (Greek) "flowing from the earth." Also means "the poppy" in Latin. Var., Rea.

Rhoda (Greek) "roses; from Rhodes." Var. and dim., Rhody, Roda, Rodi, Rodie, Rodina.

Ria (Spanish) "mouth of a river."

Rica (Teutonic) "peaceful river." Var., Ricca, Ricki, Rickie, Ricky, Riki, Rikki, Rycca.

Ricarda (Teutonic) "powerful ruler." Feminine of *Richard*. Dim., Dickie, Ric, Rica, Ricardama, Rickie, Ricky.

Rima (English) "lover of nature."

Risa (Latin) "laughter."

Rita (Greek) "a pearl." Var., Reta.

Riva (Old French) "shore." Var. and dim., Ree, Reeva, Rivalee, Rivi, Rivy.

Roanna (Latin) "sweet; gracious." Var. and dim., Ranna, Roana, Roanne, Ronni, Ronnie, Ronny.

Roberta (Teutonic) "shining fame."Feminine of *Robert*. Var. and dim., Bertie, Bobbe, Bobbette, Bobbi, Bobbie, Bobby, Bobbye, Bobina, Bobine, Bobinette, Robbi, Robbie, Robby, Robena, Robenia, Robi, Robin, Robina, Robine, Robinett, Robinette, Robinia, Ruberta, Ruperta.

Robin (English) "a robin." Var. and dim., Robbi, Robbie, Robbin, Robby, Robena, Robenia, Robi, Robina, Robine, Robinett, Robinette, Robinia, Robyn.

Rochelle (French) "little rock." Var. and dim., Roch, Rochella, Rochette, Roshelle, Shell, Shelley, Shelly.

Roderica (Teutonic) "famous princess." Feminine of *Roderick*. Dim., Rica, Rickie, Roddie, Roddy.

Rohana (Hindustani) "sweet incense."

Rolanda (Teutonic) "from the famous land." Feminine of *Roland*. Var. and dim., Orlanda, Ro, Rola, Rolande.

Roma (Latin) "wanderer; woman of Rome." Var., Romaine, Romelle, Romilda, Romina.

Romilda (Teutonic) "glorious warrior." Var. and dim., Malda, Milda, Romalda, Romelda.

Romola (Latin) "the Roman." Var. and dim., Romella, Romelle, Romie, Romy.

Ronalda (Old Norse) "very powerful" Feminine of *Ronald*. Var. and dim., Rona, Ronnie, Ronny.

Rosabel (Latin) "beautiful rose." Var., Rosabella, Rosabelle.

Rosalba (Latin) "white rose."

Roselinda (Spanish) "beautiful rose." Var. and dim., Ros, Rosalind, Rosalinde, Rosaline, Rosalyn, Rosalynd, Roselin, Roseline, Roselyn, Rosie, Roslyn, Roz, Rozalin.

Rosamond (Teutonic) "famous protector; horse-protector." Also means "pure rose" in Latin. Var. and dim., Ros, Rosamund, Rosamunda, Rosemonde, Rosemundie, Rosmunda, Roz, Rozamond, Rozamund.

Rosanna (Latin) "graceful rose." Var. and dim., Ranna, Roanna, Roanne, Rosann, Rosanne, Roseann, Roseanne, Rosian.

Rose (Greek) "a rose; love." Var. and dim., Rasia, Rhoda, Rhodia, Rhody, Rois, Rosa, Rosalee, Rosaleen, Rosalia, Rosalie, Rosaline, Rosel, Rosella, Roselle, Rosena, Rosene, Rosetta, Rosette, Rosie, Rosina, Rosita, Rosy, Rozalia, Rozalie, Roze, Rozele, Rozelle, Rozina, Zita.

Rosemarie (Hebrew) "Mary's rose; remembrance." Also means "the dew of the sea" in Latin. Var., Rose Marie, Rosemary.

Rosetta (Italian) "little rose." Var., Rosita.

Rowena (Celtic) "long white hair." Also means "famous friend" in Anglo-Saxon. Var. and dim., Ranna, Rena, Ro, Ronni, Ronnie, Ronny, Row, Rowe.

Roxane (Persian) "dawn." Var. and dim., Rosana, Rox, Roxana, Roxanna, Roxanne, Roxi, Roxie, Roxine, Roxy.

Ruby (Latin) "the gem ruby; red." Var. and dim., Rubetta, Rubi, Rubia, Rubie, Rubina.

Rudelle (Teutonic) "fame." Var., Ruda.

Rue (Greek) "herb of grace." Var., Reu, Rhu.

Rufina (Greek) "red-haired." Feminine of *Rufus.*

Ruth (Hebrew) "beautiful friend; compassionate." Var. and dim., Ruthe, Ruthi, Ruthie.

S

Saba (Greek) "woman of Sheba."

Sabina (Latin) "a Sabine woman."Var. and dim., Bina, Sabine, Savina.

Sabra (Hebrew) "to rest."

Sabrina (Latin) "from the boundary." Also means "a princess" in Anglo-Saxon. Var. and dim., Brina, Zabrina.

Sacha (Greek) "helper of mankind." Russian feminine of *Alexander*.

Sadira (Persian) "the lotus tree; dreamy." Also means "an ostrich returning from the water" in Arabic. Var. and dim., Dira, Sadirah, Sadiras.

Salina (Greek) "salty." Var., Salena.

Salome (Hebrew) "peace; tranquility." Var. and dim., Loma, Sally, Saloma, Salomé, Salomi.

Salvia (Latin) "sage; fragrant herb." Var., Salva, Salvina.

Samantha (Aramaic) "listener; attentive." Dim., Sam, Sama, Sammy.

Samara (Hebrew) "protected by God." Dim., Mara, Sam, Sammy.

Samuela (Hebrew) "name of God." Feminine of *Samuel*. Var. and dim., Ela, Sam, Samantha, Samela, Samella, Sammy, Samuella, Uella.

Sancia (Latin) "sacred; inviolate." Var., Sancha, Sanchia.

Sandra (Greek) "helper of mankind." Feminine of *Alexander*. Dim., Sandi, Sandy, Sandye.

Sapphire (Greek) "sapphire gem; sapphire blue." Also means "beautiful" in Hebrew. Var. and dim., Phira, Saphra, Sapphira, Sephira.

Sarah (Hebrew) "princess." Var. and dim., Sadella, Sadie, Sadye, Saidee, Sal, Salaidh, Sallee, Salli, Sallie, Sally, Sara, Sarena, Sarene, Saretta, Sarette, Sari, Sarine, Sarita, Sayre, Shara, Sharai, Shari, Sharon, Sharona, Sher, Sheree, Sheri, Sherie, Sherri, Sherrie, Sherry, Sherye, Sorcha, Sydel, Sydelle, Zara, Zarah, Zaria.

Sarita (Hebrew) "little princess." Var., Saretta.

Savanna (Old Spanish) "from the mesa, or open plain."

Scarlett (Middle English) "scarlet color."

Sebastiana (Greek) "grand; revered." Feminine of *Sebastian*. Var., Sebastiane, Sebastienne.

Secunda (Latin) "second-born."

Sela (Hebrew) "a rock."

Selena (Greek) "the moon." Var. and dim., Celene, Celie, Celina, Celinda, Celine, Lena, Salene, Sela, Selene, Selia, Selie, Selina, Selinda, Seline, Sena.

Selima (Hebrew) "peaceful." Arabic feminine of *Solomon*. Var., Selimah.

Selma (Teutonic) "protected; divine helmet." Also means "fair" in Celtic. Feminine of *Anselm*. Var., Anselma, Zelma.

Semele (Latin) "one time only." Var., Semela.

Senalda (Spanish) "an omen." Dim., Alda, Enalda, Sena.

Septima (Latin) "seventh-born."

Seraphina (Hebrew) "burning; ardent." Var. and dim., Sera, Serafina, Serafine, Seraphine.

Serena (Latin) "serene; calm; tranquil; peaceful." Var. and dim., Reena, Rena, Serene, Sirene.

Serilda (Teutonic) "armored maid of war." Var. and dim., Rilda, Sarilda.

Sharon (Hebrew) "the plain of Sharon; fertility; exotic beauty." Var. and dim., Shara, Sharai, Shari, Sharona, Sharry, Sherri, Sherrie, Sherry, Sherye.

Sheba (Hebrew) "from Sheba; daughter of our pledge." Var., Saba.

Sheena (Irish) "God's gift."

Sheila (Latin) "blind." Also means "musical" in Celtic. Var. and dim., Seila, Selia, Sheela, Sheelagh, Sheelah, Sheilah, Shelagh, Shelley, Shelli, Shellie, Shelly.

Shelah (Hebrew) "requested." Var. and dim., Shaya, Shea, Shela, Sheya.

Shelley (Old English) "shelly island." Var. and dim., Shell, Shelli, Shellie, Shelly.

Sherry (French) "cherished." Var. and dim., Sher, Sheree, Sheri, Sherri, Sherrie, Sherye.

Shirley (Anglo-Saxon) "from the white meadow." Var. and dim., Sher, Sheree, Sheri, Sherill, Sherline, Sherri, Sherrie, Sherry, Sherye, Sheryl, Shir, Shirlee, Shirleen, Shirlene, Shirline.

Shoshana (Hebrew) "rose." Var., Shoshannah.

Sibyl (Greek) "prophetess; wise." Var. and dim., Cybil, Cybill, Sib, Sibbie, Sibby, Sibeal, Sibel, Sibell, Sibella, Sibelle, Sibilla, Sibley, Sibyll, Sibylla, Sibylle, Sybil, Sybila, Sybilla, Sybille.

Sidonia (Phoenician) "ensnare." Also means "linen" in Greek. Var., Sadonia, Sidonie.

Sidra (Latin) "of the stars; shining." Var., Siddra, Sidras.

Sigfreda (Old German) "victory; fulfillment; inward peace." Feminine of *Siegfried*.

Simone (Hebrew) "one who hears." Feminine of *Simon*. Var. and dim., Simona, Simonetta, Simonette, Simonne.

Sirena (Greek) "a siren; fatally beautiful temptress."

Solita (Latin) "tranquil solitude." Var. and dim., Lita, Sola, Solitta.

Sondra (Greek) "one who helps mankind."

Sonia (Greek) "stranger." Var. and dim., Sonja, Sonni, Sonnie, Sonny, Sonya, Sunny.

Sophia (Greek) "wisdom." Var. and dim., Sofia, Sofie, Sonia, Sonja, Sonni, Sonnie, Sonny, Sonya, Soph, Sophey, Sophi, Sophie, Sophonisba, Sophronia, Sophy, Sunny.

Sophronia (Greek) "wise; sensible; discerning." Var., Sonja, Sonya.

Sorcha (Gaelic) "bright."

Spring (Old English) "springtime."

Stacey (Greek) "one who shall rise again; resurrection; immortality." Var. and dim., Stace, Stacia, Stacie, Stacy.

Star (Anglo-Saxon) "star." Var., Starr.

Stella (Latin) "a star." Dim., Stel.

Stephanie (Greek) "a crown; garland." Feminine of *Stephen*. Var. and dim., Stefa, Stefana, Stefania, Stefanie, Steffi, Steffie, Stepha, Stephana, Stephani, Stephania, Stéphanie, Stephenie, Stephi, Stephie, Stesha, Stevana, Stevena, Stevie.

Storm (Old English) "stormy; tempestuous." Dim., Stormi, Stormie, Stormy.

Sunny (English) "sunny; cheerful."

Susan (Hebrew) "a lily." Var. and dim., Siusan, Sosanna, Sue, Sukey, Suki, Susana, Susanetta, Susanna, Susannah, Susanne, Suse, Susette, Susi, Susie, Susy, Suzanna,

Suzanne, Suzelle, Suzetta, Suzette, Suzi, Suzie, Suzy, Zsa Zsa.

Swanhilda (Teutonic) "swan battle-maiden." Var., Swanhild.

Sydelle (Hebrew) "enchantress." Var., Sydel.

Sydney (Hebrew) "enticer." Also means "from St. Denis" in Old French. Feminine of *Sidney*. Var. and dim., Sid, Sidney, Sidonia, Sidonie, Syd.

Sylvia (Latin) "maiden of the forest." Feminine of *Silvanus*. Var. and dim., Silva, Silvana, Silvia, Silvie, Syl, Sylva, Sylvana, Sylvie, Zilvia.

T

Tabitha (Aramaic) "the gazelle; graceful." Dim., Tabbi, Tabbie, Tabby.

Tacita (Latin) "silent."

Talia (Greek) "blooming." Var. and dim., Tallie, Tally, Thalia.

Talitha (Aramaic) "damsel." Var., Taletha.

Tallulah (American Indian) "leaping water; vivacious." Var. and dim., Tallie, Tallou, Tallu, Tallula, Tally.

Tama (Hebrew) "astonishment." Var., Tamah.

Tamara (Hebrew) "palm tree." Var. and dim., Tama, Tamar, Tamma, Tammi, Tammie, Tammy.

Tammy (Hebrew) "perfection." Dim., Tammi, Tammie.

Tansy (Latin) "tenacious; persistent."

Tara (Gaelic) "rocky tower; crag; ancient capital of Irish kings."

Tempest (Old French) "tempestuous; stormy."

Tertia (Latin) "third-born." Var. and dim., Teria, Terias, Terza, Tia.

Tessa (Greek) "fourth-born." Dim., Tess, Tessi, Tessie, Tessy.

Thaddea (Greek) "praised; brave." Feminine of *Thaddeus*. Var. and dim., Thada, Thadda, Thadine.

Thais (Greek) "the bond."

Thalassa (Greek) "from the sea."

Thea (Greek) "divine; extraordinarily beautiful."

Thecia (Greek) "divine fame." Var., Thekla.

Theda (Greek) "God's gift."

Thelma (Greek) "a nursling." Dim., Thel.

Themis (Greek) "justice." Var. and dim., Tema, Thema.

Theodora (Greek) "divine gift of God." Feminine of *Theodore*. Var. and dim., Dora, Dori, Fedora, Feodora, Ted, Tedda, Teddi, Teddie, Teddy, Tedi, Tedra, Teodora, Thea, Theda, Thia, Thekla, Theo, Theodora.

Theodosia (Greek) "God-given." Var. and dim., Dosia, Dosie, Feodosia, Teodosia, Theda.

Theola (Greek) "one who speaks with God; divine gift from heaven." Dim., Lola, Theo.

Theone (Greek) "divine."

Theophila (Greek) "beloved of God." Var., Teophila.

Theora (Greek) "meditator."

Thera (Greek) "untamed; wild."

Theresa (Greek) "the reaper." Var. and dim., Tera, Teresa, Terese, Teresita, Teressa, Teri, Terra, Terri, Terrie, Terry, Terrye, Tess, Tessa, Tessi, Tessie, Tessy, Therese, Thérese, Tracey, Tracie, Tracy, Tresa, Trescha, Zita.

Thetis (Greek) "resolute."

Thirza (Hebrew) "pleasant." Var., Thyrza, Tirza.

Thisbe (Greek) "from the place of the doves."

Thomasina (Aramaic) "a twin." Feminine of *Thomas*. Var. and dim., Tammi, Tammie, Tamzin, Thomasa. Thomasin, Thomasine, Toma, Tomasina, Tomasine, Tommi, Tommie, Tommy.

Thora (Old Norse) "thunder." Feminine of *Thor*. Var. and dim., Thordia, Thoris, Tyra.

Thorberta (Old Norse) "brilliance."

Thyra (Greek) "one who carries a shield."

Tiberia (Latin) "of the Tiber river." Dim., Tibbie, Tibby.

Tiffany (Greek) "the aspect of God." Var. and dim., Tifanie, Tiff, Tiffa, .Tiffi, Tiffie, Tiffy.

Tilda (Teutonic) "mighty in battle." Dim, Tildi, Tildie, Tildy.

Timothea (Greek) "honoring God." Feminine of *Timothy*. Var. and dim., Thea, Tim, Timi, Timmi, Timmie, Timmy, Timotea.

Tita (Latin) "a title of honor."

Titania (Greek) "titan; giant." Dim., Tania, Tita.

Toby (Hebrew) "God is good." Feminine of *Tobias*. Var. and dim., Tobe, Tobey, Tobi, Tobye, Tova, Tove, Tybi, Tybie.

Toni (Latin) "beyond worth or praise." Var., Tonia, Tonie, Toinette.

Topaz (Latin) "the topaz gem." Var., Topaza.

Tourmaline (Singhalese) "the tourmaline gem."

Tracy (Latin) "courageous; bold." Var., Tracey, Tracie.

Trilby (Italian) "to sing with trills; frivolous." Dim., Trilbi, Trill, Trilly.

Trina (Greek) "purity." Var. and dim., Trenna, Trinee, Trinia.

Trinette (Greek) "little pure one." Var. and dim., Rinee, Trinatte, Trini.

Trista (Latin) "sorrowful." Feminine of *Tristan*. Dim., Tris, Tristas.

Trixie (Latin) "blessing; one who brings happiness." Var. and dim., Trissie, Trix, Trixi, Trixy.

Trudy (Old German) "loved one." Var., Truda, Trudel, Trudi, Trudie.

True (English) "true."

Tuesday (Old English) "born on Tuesday."

Tullia (Gaelic) "peaceful; serene; quiet." Feminine of *Tully*.

U

Udele (Anglo-Saxon) "very wealthy." Var., Uda, Udelle.

Ula (Teutonic) "heir to an estate." Means "jewel of the sea" in Celtic. Var., Eula, Ula, Ulla, Ylla.

Ulrica (Teutonic) "ruler of all." Feminine of *Ulric*. Var. and dim., Ulrika, Rica.

Ulva (Gothic) "the wolf; courage."

Una (Latin) "one." Means "famine" in Celtic. Var., Ona, Oona.

Undine (Latin) "a wave; water-sprite." Var., Ondine.

Urania (Greek) "heavenly." Var. and dim., Rania, Ranie, Urana, Uranie.

Uria (Hebrew) "the light of God." Feminine of *Uriah*. Var. and dim., Ria, Uri, Uriah, Urial, Urissa.

Ursa (Latin) "she-bear."

Ursel (Latin) "little she-bear."

Ursula (Latin) "she-bear; fearless." Var. and dim., Nullie, Orsa, Orsola, Ursa, Ursala, Ursel, Ursi, Ursie, Ursola, Ursule, Ursulette, Ursulina, Ursuline, Ursy.

Uta (Teutonic) "battle heroine."

V

Vala (Gothic) "chosen one."

Valda (Teutonic) "heroine of battle." Var. and dim., Val, Velda.

Valeda (Latin) "vigorous; sound of body." Var. and dim., Aleda, Leda, Vala, Vale, Valeta.

Valentina (Latin) "valiant; healthy; strong." Var. and dim., Teena, Tina, Val, Vale, Valeda, Valencia, Valentia, Valentine, Valera, Valeria, Valerie, Valida, Valli, Vallie, Vally, Valora.

Valerie (Latin) "valorous; strong." Var. and dim., Val, Valaree, Vale, Valeria, Valérie, Valery, Valerye, Valli, Vallie, Vally, Valoree.

Valonia (Latin) "from the vale or valley." Var. and dim., Val, Vallonia, Valoniah.

Valora (Latin) "valorous."

Vanessa (Greek) "butterfly." Var. and dim., Nessa, Nessi, Nessie, Nessy, Van, Vania, Vanna Vanni, Vannie, Vanny.

Vania (Hebrew) "gift of God." Russian feminine of *John*. Dim., Van.

Vanora (Old Welsh) "white wave."

Varina (Greek) "stranger."

Vashti (Persian) "beautiful." Var. and dim., Ashti, Vastha, Vasthia, Vasti.

Veda (Sanskrit) "knowledge; wisdom." Var., Vedis.

Vega (Arabic) "falling star."

Velda (Teutonic) "wisdom of inspiration." Var., Valeda, Veleda.

Velika (Slavic) "one who is great."

Velma (Teutonic) "firm protector; the helmet." Feminine of *William*. Var., Vilma.

Velvet (Middle English) "velvet."

Ventura (Spanish) "good fortune."

Venus (Latin) "beautiful;" The Roman goddess of beauty. Dim., Venita, Vin, Vinita, Vinnie, Vinny.

Vera (Latin) "true." Also means "faith" in Russian. Var. and dim., Veradis, Vere, Verena, Verene, Verina, Verine, Verla, Verra.

Verbena (Latin) "the flower verbena." Var. and dim., Bena, Benia, Verbenia.

Verda (Latin) "fresh; new." Dim., Verdie.

Verena (Old German) "guardian."

Verna (Latin) "vernal; born in the spring." Feminine of *Vernon*. Var. and dim., Verda, Verena, Verne, Verneta, Vernice, Vernis, Vernita, Virina, Virna.

Veronica (Latin-Greek) "true image." Var. and dim., Ranna, Ronni, Ronnie, Ronny, Vera, Veronika, Veronike, Véronique, Vonni, Vonnie, Vonny.

Vespera (Latin) "evening star."

Vesta (Latin) "homebody." The Roman goddess of the hearth. Dim., Esta.

Victoria (Latin) "victorious." Feminine of *Victor*. Var. and dim., Vic, Vicki, Vickie, Vicky, Victoire, Victorie, Victorine, Vikki, Vikky, Vitoria, Vittoria.

Vida (Hebrew) "beloved one." Feminine of *David*. Var. and dim., Davida, Vidda, Viddah, Vidette,

Vidonia (Portuguese) "branch of a vine."

Vigilia (Latin) "alert; watchful; vigilant."

Vignette (French) "small vine."

Vincentia (Latin) "conquering." Feminine of *Vincent*. Var., Vincenta.

Vinita (Latin) "woman from Venice." Var., Venita.

Vinna (Anglo-Saxon) "of the vine." Var., Vina, Vina, Vine.

Violet (Latin) "the flower violet; shy." Var. and dim., Eolande, Iolande, Iolanthe, Vi, Viola, Violante, Viole, Violetta, Violette, Vye, Yolanda, Yolande, Yolane, Yolanthe.

Virgilia (Latin) "thriving; bearer of rod or staff." Feminine of *Virgil*.

Virginia (Latin) "virginal; gaining poise and power." Var. and dim., Ginger, Ginni, Ginnie, Ginny, Jinny, Virg, Virgie, Virgilia, Virgini, Virginie, Virgy.

Viridas (Latin) "blooming; young."

Vita (Latin) "life; lively." Var., Veta, Vida, Vitia.

Vivian (Latin) "full of life."Var. and dim., Vevay, Vi, Viv, Vivi, Vivia, Viviana, Viviane, Vivianne, Vivie, Vivien, Vivienne, Vivyan.

Voleta (Old French) "veiled." Var., Voletta.

W

Wahkuna (American Indian) "beautiful." Var., Wakkuna.

Walda (Old German) "leader." Feminine of *Waldo*. Var., Waldo, Welda.

Wallis (Old English) "from Wales." Feminine of *Wallace*. Dim., Wallie, Wally.

Wanda (Teutonic) "wanderer." Var. and dim., Vanda, Wandie, Wandis, Wenda, Wendeline, Wendi, Wendie, Wendy, Wendye.

Wanetta (Anglo-Saxon) "fair one." Var., Wannett.

Warda (Old German) "watchwoman; protector." Feminine of *Ward*. Var., Wardena.

Welcome (Anglo-Saxon) "welcome; greet gladly."

Wendelin (Teutonic) "wandering; wending one's way." Var. and dim., Wende, Wendelina, Wendeline, Wendie, Wendolyn, Wendy.

Wendy (Old Welsh) "white-browed; fair complexioned. Var., Wenda, Wendeline, Wendi, Wendie, Wendye.

Wenona (American Indian) "first-born." Var., Wanonah, Wenoa, Wenonah, Winona.

Wesla (Old English) "from the west meadow." Feminine of *Wesley*. Var. and dim., Wes, Wesa, Wesle, Weslee, Wesley.

Wilda (Anglo-Saxon) "wild; uncivilized." Var. and dim., Wilde, Wildee.

Wilfreda (Teutonic) "peacemaker." Feminine of *Wilfred*. Var. and dim., Freda, Wildfreda.

Wilhelmina (Teutonic) "firm protectress." Feminine of *William*. Var. and dim., Billi, Billie, Billy, Guglielma, Guilema, Guillelmina, Guillelmine, Guillemette, Helma, Mimi, Min, Mina, Minna, Minni, Minnie, Minny, Valma, Velma, Vilhelmina, Vilma, Wileen, Wilhelma, Wilhelmine, Willa, Willabel, Willabella, Willamina, Willeta, Willette, Willi, Williamina, Willie, Willy, Wilma, Wilmet, Wilmette, Wylma.

Wilona (Anglo-Saxon) "desirable." Var., Wilone.

Winema (American Indian) "female chief."

Winifred (Teutonic) "friend in peace." Also means "white wave" in Welsh. Var. and dim., Fredi, Freddi, Freddie, Freddy, Ona, Oona, Una, Win, Winfried, Winnie, Winnifred, Winny.

Winola (Old German) "gracious; friendly."

Wynne (Celtic) "fair; white." Var. and dim., Winnie, Winny, Wyne.

X

Xanthe (Greek) "fair-haired." Var., Xantha.

Xaviera (Arabic) "bright." Also means "new house" in Spanish Basque. Feminine of *Xavier*.

Xenia (Greek) "hospitable." Var., Xena, Zena, Zenia.

Xylia (Greek) "of the woods." Var., Xylina.

Xylona (Greek) "from the forest."

Y

Yedda (Old English) "songstress." Var., Yetta.

Yetta (Old English) "benefactress." Var. and dim., Yedda, Yeta, Yetti.

Yolanda (Greek) "the violet flower; modest." Var. and dim., Eolande, Iolande, Iolanthe, Yolande, Yolane, Yolanthe.

Yseult (Celtic) "the fair."

Yvonne (Old French) "user of the yew-bow." Feminine of *Ivar*. Var. and dim., Evonne, Ivonne, Von, Vonnie, Yevette, Yvette.

Z

Zabrina (Anglo-Saxon) "of noble birth." Var. and dim., Brina, Zabrine.

Zandra (Greek) "helper of mankind." Feminine of *Alexander*.

Zara (Hebrew) "morning light."

Zea (Latin) "like ripe grain."

Zebada (Hebrew) "God's gift." Feminine of *Zebadiah*. Dim., Zeba.

Zena (Persian) "woman." Also means "hospitable" in Greek. Var. and dim., Zeena, Zenecia, Zenia, Zenija, Zina.

Zenobia (Arabic) "father's pride." Also means "born of Zeus" in Greek. Var. and dim., Zena, Zenaida, Zenda, Zenia, Zenna, Zénobie.

Zera (Hebrew) "seeds."

Zerelda (Teutonic) "battle-maiden." Var., Serilda, Zeralda.

Zerlina (Teutonic) "calm; beautiful." Var. and dim., Zerla, Zerlinda, Zerline.

Zeta (Greek) "the letter Z."

Zillah (Hebrew) "shadow; image." Var., Zilla.

Zinnia (Latin) "the zinnia flower." Var., Zinia.

Zipporah (Hebrew) "sparrow." Var. and dim., Ceporah, Tippi, Tippie, Tsiporah, Zippora.

Zita (Celtic) "seductive." Var. and dim., Zitah, Zitella.

Zoe (Greek) "life." Var., Zoe.

Zora (Slavic) "dawn." Var. and dim., Zarya, Zohra, Zorah, Zorana, Zorina, Zorine.

Zuleika (Arabic) "the fair one."

MALE NAMES LISTING

Aaron
Abbot
Abel
Abelard
Abiezer
Abner
Abraham
Adair
Adam
Addison
Adiel
Adin
Adolph
Adrian
Alan
Alban
Albert
Alden
Aldo
Aldous
Alexander
Alfred
Alger
Algernon
Alphonse
Alston
Alvin
Ambert
Ambrose
Amos

Anatole
Andrew
Angelo
Angus
Anselm
Anson
Anthony
Archibald
Arden
Argus
Arnold
Arthur
Arvin
Asa
Asher
Ashford
Aubrey
August
Averill
Avery
Axel
Aylwin

Baird
Baldwin
Bancroft
Banning
Barnaby
Barret
Barry

Bartholomew
Barton
Baructt
Basil
Baxter
Beau
Benedict
Benjamin
Benton
Berkeley
Bernard
Bertram
Bevan
Bing
Birkett
Birley
Bishop
Blade
Blaine
Blair
Blake
Blaze
Boden
Booth
Boris
Bowen
Boyd
Brad
Bradford
Bradley
Bran
Brant
Brendan
Brent

Brett
Brian
Brice
Broderick
Bronson
Bruce
Bruno
Buck
Budd
Burgess
Burke
Burl
Burton
Byron

Cadmar
Cadmus
Caesar
Caleb
Calvert
Calvin
Cameron
Carey
Carleton
Carlisle
Carroll
Carson
Carter
Caspar
Cass
Cassidy
Castor
Cato
Cecil

Cedric
Chad
Charles
Chauncey
Chester
Christian
Christopher
Clarence
Clark
Claude
Clayton
Clement
Clifford
Clifton
Clinton
Clive
Clyde
Coleman
Colin
Conan
Conrad
Constantine
Corey
Cormac
Cornelius
Corydon
Cosmo
Courtney
Craig
Crosby
Curtis
Cuthbert
Cyril
Cyrus

Dacey
Dagan
Dagwood
Dalbert
Dale
Dallas
Dalton
Daly
Damon
Dana
Daniel
Darcy
Darius
Darnell
Darrell
Darren
David
Davin
Dean
Delbert
Delmar
Demas
Demetrius
Dempsey
Dermot
Derrick
Derry
Derwin
Desmond
Devin
Dewey
Dewitt
Dexter
Dillon

Dixon
Dolan
Dominic
Donald
Dorian
Douglas
Drew
Dudley
Duke
Duncan
Dunstan
Durand
Durward
Dwayne
Dwight
Dylan

Earl
Eaton
Ebenezer
Edan
Edgar
Edmund
Edward
Edwin
Egan
Egbert
Elbert
Eldon
Eleazer
Eli
Elias
Elisha
Ellery
Ellison
Elmer
Elmo
Elmore
Elroy
Elwin
Elwood
Emanuel
Emil
Emmett
Emory
Enoch
Ephraim
Eric
Ernest
Erwin
Esmond
Ethan
Eugene
Evan
Everett
Ezekiel
Ezra

Fabian
Fairfax
Falkner
Farand
Farrell
Felix
Ferdinand
Fergus
Firman
Flavian

Fletcher
Flint
Floyd
Flynn
Forrester
Francis
Franklin
Frederick
Fremont
Fulton

Gabriel
Gabel
Gale
Galen
Galvin
Gamaliel
Gamel
Gannon
Gardiner
Garfield
Garland
Garett
Garner
Garnet
Garrick
Garvey
Gary
Gavin
Geoffrey
George
Gerald
Germain
Gershom
Gervas
Gideon
Gifford
Gilbert
Giles
Gilmore
Gilroy
Glen
Goddard
Godwin
Gordon
Graham
Grant
Grayson
Gregory
Griffith
Griswold
Gunther
Gustave
Guy

Hadden
Hadrian
Hadwin
Hagen
Haines
Halbert
Halden
Hale
Halsey
Halstead
Hamilton
Hamish
Hamlet

Hamlin
Hamon
Hanley
Hannibal
Hans
Hansel
Harcourt
Harden
Harding
Hardy
Harlan
Harley
Harlow
Harmon
Harold
Harper
Harrison
Harvey
Hawley
Haydon
Hayes
Heath
Heathcliff
Hector
Heman
Henry
Herbert
Herman
Heywood
Hezekiah
Hilary
Hillel
Hilliard
Hilton

Hiram
Hiroshi
Hobart
Holden
Hollis
Homer
Horace
Hosea
Howard
Howell
Hubert
Humbert
Humphrey
Hyman

Ian
Ichabod
Ignatius
Igor
Ingmar
Ira
Irving
Isaac
Isidore
Isaiah
Ishmael
Israel
Ivan
Ivar

Jaaziniah
Jabez
Jack
Jacob
Jairus

James
Japhet
Jared
Jason
Jasper
Jay
Jed
Jeffrey
Jeremy
Jerome
Jesse
Jethro
Joab
Joachim
Joel
John
Jonah
Jonathan
Joseph
Joshua
Josiah
Jotham
Judah
Julius
Justin

Kane
Kay
Keith
Kelly
Keisey
Kenard
Kendall
Kenneth
Kenyon
Kermit
Kerwin
Kester
Kevin
Kimbal
Kirby
Kirk
Konstantin
Kyle

Lachlan
Lamar
Lambert
Lamont
Lancelot
Langston
Lars
Larson
Latimer
Lawrence
Lee
Leif
Lemuel
Leo
Leonard
Leopold
Leroy
Leslie
Lester
Lewis
Lindsay
Linus
Lionel

Lloyd
Logan
Lowell
Lucius
Luke
Luther
Lyle
Lyndon

Madoc
Madison
Magnus
Major
Malcom
Malise
Mallory
Malvin
Manasseh
Manchu
Manfred
Manley
Manuel
Manville
Marcellus
Mario
Mark
Marlin
Marley
Marlow
Marmaduke
Marmion
Marsden
Marshall
Martial
Martin
Marvin
Mason
Mato
Matthew
Maurice
Maximilian
Maxwell
Mayor
Maynard
Meade
Meredith
Merle
Meyer
Micah
Michael
Miles
Millard
Milo
Milton
Mitchell
Monroe
Mongtomery
Montague
Morgan
Morley
Morris
Mortimer
Morton
Moses
Murdoch
Murray
Myron

Nathan
Nathanial
Neal
Nelson
Nicholas
Nigel
Noah
Noble
Noel
Norman
Norton

Oakley
Obadiah
Octavius
Odell
Ogden
Olaf
Oliver
Omar
Oren
Orion
Orson
Orval
Orvin
Osbert
Oscar
Oswald
Otis
Otto
Ovid
Owen
Ozias

Page
Paine
Palmer
Parnell
Patrick
Paul
Percival
Perry
Peter
Philip
Plato
Powell
Preston

Quentin
Quillan
Quincy
Quinn

Rad
Radcliff
Radolf
Ralph
Ramsey
Randolf
Raphael
Raymond
Regan
Reginald
René
Reuben
Rex
Rexford
Reynard

Rhett
Richard
Richmond
Rider
Ridgley
Ridley
Riley
Ring
Riordan
Rip
Ripley
Roald
Roarke
Robert
Rochester
Rockwell
Roderick
Rodman
Rodney
Roger
Roland
Romeo
Ronald
Rooney
Rory
Roscoe
Ross
Roy
Royce
Rudolph
Rudyard
Rufus
Russell
Rutherford
Ryan

Salvador
Sam
Samson
Samuel
Sanborn
Sancho
Sanders
Sanford
Sargent
Saul
Sawyer
Saxon
Schuyler
Scott
Sebastian
Sedgwick
Selby
Seldon
Selwyn
Serge
Seth
Seton
Seward
Sewell
Sexton
Seymour
Shandy
Shannon
Shaw
Sheehan
Sheffield
Sheldon

Shelley
Shepherd
Sherard
Sheridan
Sherlock
Sherman
Sherwin
Sherwood
Sidney
Siegfried
Sigmund
Sigurd
Silvanus
Silvester
Simon
Sinclair
Skip
Sloan
Smith
Sol
Solomon
Solon
Somerset
Spencer
Sprague
Stacy
Stafford
Standish
Standfield
Stanford
Stanhope
Stanislaus
Stanley
Stanton
Stanwood
Stedman
Stephen
Sterling
Sterne
Stewart
Stillman
Stoddard
Styles
Sumner
Sutton
Swain

Tab
Talbot
Tanner
Tate
Tavis
Taylor
Teague
Tearle
Tedman
Templeton
Terence
Terrell
Thaddeus
Thane
Thatcher
Thayer
Theobald
Theodore
Theodoric
Theron
Thomas

Thor
Thorald
Thorley
Thorndike
Thornton
Thorpe
Thurlow
Thurman
Thurston
Tiffany
Tilden
Tilford
Timothy
Titus
Tobias
Todd
Toland
Torrance
Townsend
Tracy
Trahern
Travers
Tremayne
Trent
Trevor
Tristan
Tristram
Troy
Truman
Tucker
Tully
Turner
Tybalt
Tyler
Tynan
Tyrone
Tyson

Udell
Ulric
Ulysses
Upton
Urban
Uriah

Vachel
Vail
Val
Valentine
Valerian
Van
Vance
Varden
Varian
Vaughn
Vere
Vernon
Victor
Vincent
Vinson
Virgil
Vito
Vivian
Vladimir
Volney

Wade
Wadsworth
Wainwright

Waite
Wakefield
Walcott
Waldermar
Walden
Waldo
Waldron
Walford
Walker
Wallace
Wallmond
Walter
Walton
Ward
Ware
Warfield
Warford
Waring
Warner
Warren
Warwick
Washburn
Washington
Watson
Waverly
Wayland
Wayne
Webb
Webster
Welby
Weldon
Welford
Wellington
Wells
Wendell
Wesley
Westcott
Weston
Whitby
Whitelaw
Whitford
Whitney
Whittaker
Wilbur
Wiley
Wilford
Wilfred
Willard
William
Willis
Willoughby
Wilmer
Wilmot
Wilson
Wilton
Winchell
Windsor
Winfield
Winfred
Winslow
Winston
Winthrop
Wirt
Wolcott
Wolf
Wolfgang
Wolfram

Woodley
Woodrow
Woodward
Worth
Wright
Wyatt
Wylie
Wyman
Wyndham
Wynn
Wystan

Xanthus
Xavier
Xenophon
Xenos
Xerxes
Ximenes

Yale
Yancy
Yates
Yehudi
York
Yule
Yves

Zachary
Zared
Zebadiah
Zebulon
Zedekiah
Zenas
Zephaniah

FEMALE NAMES LISTING

Abigail
Ada
Adah
Adelaide
Adeline
Adine
Adora
Adrienne
Agatha
Agnes
Aileen
Aimee
Alana
Alarice
Alberta
Alda
Aletheia
Alexandra
Alfreda
Alice
Allegra
Alma
Almira
Alta
Althea
Alva
Alvina
Amanda
Amber
Amelia
Amena
Aminta
Amity
Amy
Anastasia
Anatola
Andrea
Angela
Anita
Ann
Anthea
Antonia
April
Arabella
Ardis
Ariadine
Arlene
Astra
Astrid
Atalanta
Athena
Audrey
Augusta
Aurelia
Aurora
Avis
Aviva

Barbara
Beata

Beatrice
Belinda
Bena
Benedicta
Bernadine
Bernice
Bertha
Beryl
Beth
Bethia
Beulah
Beverly
Billie
Blanche
Blythe
Bonnie
Brenda
Brenna
Bridget
Brunhilde

Calliope
Callista
Camilla
Candace
Cara
Carla
Carmel
Carmen
Carol
Caroline
Cassandra
Cecilia
Celeste
Celia
Chandra
Charis
Charity
Charlotte
Charmaine
Cherie
Chloe
Chloris
Christine
Clara
Clarabelle
Clarissa
Claudia
Clementine
Cleopatra
Clotilda
Colette
Colinette
Colleen
Constance
Consuela
Cora
Cordelia
Cornelia
Cymbeline
Cynara
Cynthia

Dagmar
Daisy
Dale
Dama
Damaris
Daphne

Dara
Darlene
Davina
Dawn
Deanna
Deborah
Decima
Deirdre
Delilah
Della
Delphne
Denise
Desiré
Diana
Dinah
Dione
Dixie
Dolores
Donna
Dora
Dorcas
Dorene
Doris
Dorothy
Drusilla
Dulcie

Eartha
Easter
Ebba
Echo
Eda
Edana
Eden
Edina
Edith
Edlyn
Edmonda
Edna
Edrea
Edwardine
Edwina
Effie
Eglantine
Eileen
Elaine
Elata
Eldora
Eldrida
Eleanor
Electra
Elena
Elfrida
Elga
Elise
Elissa
Eliza
Elizabeth
Ellen
Ellice
Elma
Elmira
Eloise
Elrica
Elsa
Elva
Elvina
Elvira

Elysia
Emeline
Emerald
Emily
Emina
Emlyn
Emma
Emogene
Ena
Engelberta
Enid
Enrica
Erda
Erica
Erin
Erline
Erma
Erna
Ernestine
Esme
Esmeralda
Estelle
Esther
Estrella
Ethel
Ethelinda
Etta
Eudocia
Eudora
Eugenia
Eulalia
Eunice
Euphemia
Eurydice

Eustacia
Evadne
Evangeline
Eve
Evelyn

Fabia
Faith
Fanchon
Fancy
Fanny
Farica
Farrah
Faustina
Fawn
Fay
Fayette
Fedora
Felice
Fenella
Fern
Fernanda
Fidelia
Fifi
Filma
Fiona
Flavia
Fleta
Flora
Florence
Florida
Florina
Fonda
Fortuna

Frances
Freda
Fredella
Frederica
Freya
Fulvia

Gabrielle
Gail
Galatea
Gardenia
Garland
Garnet
Gay
Gazella
Gelasia
Gemma
Gene
Geneva
Genevieve
Georgia
Georgiana
Geraldine
Gerda
Germaine
Gertrude
Gilberta
Gilda
Gillian
Gina
Ginger
Giselle
Githa
Gladys
Gleda
Glenna
Gloria
Glynis
Godiva
Golda
Grace
Greer
Greta
Griselda
Guinevere
Gunhilda
Gustava
Gwen
Gwendolyn
Gwyneth
Gypsy

Hagar
Haidee
Haldana
Halfrida
Halimeda
Hallie
Hana
Hannah
Happy
Haralda
Harmony
Harriet
Hazel
Heather
Hebe
Hedda

Hedwig
Hedy
Heidi
Helen
Helga
Helma
Heloise
Henrietta
Hera
Hermia
Hermina
Hermione
Hermosa
Hertha
Hesper
Hester
Hilary
Hilda
Hildegarde
Hildreth
Hilma
Holly
Honey
Honora
Hope
Horatia
Hortense
Hoshi
Huberta
Huette
Hulda
Hyacinth
Hypatia

Ianthe
Ida
Idalia
Idele
Idona
Ignatia
Ileana
Ilka
Ilona
Ilsa
Imogene
Ina
Inez
Inga
Ingrid
Iola
Iolanthe
Ione
Irene
Ireta
Iris
Irma
Irvette
Isa
Isabel
Isadora
Isis
Isleen
Isolde
Ita
Iva
Ivana
Ivy

Jacinda
Jacoba
Jacqueline
Jade
Jane
Jasmine
Jay
Jean
Jemima
Jennifer
Jessica
Jewel
Jill
Joan
Jobina
Jocelyn
Joletta
Josephine
Jovita
Joy
Joyce
Judith
Julia
June
Juno
Justine

Kali
Kalila
Kama
Kamaria
Kameko
Kara
Karel
Karen
Karla
Kate
Katherine
Kathleen
Kay
Keely
Keiko
Kelda
Kelly
Kendra
Kerry
Ketura
Keziah
Kim
Kimberly
Kineta
Kirby
Kirstin
Kora
Koren
Kyla
Kyna

Lacey
Lala
Lalage
Lalita
Lana
Lanette
Lani
Lara
Laraine
Larissa

Lark
Laura
Laurel
Lauren
Leveda
Laverne
Lavinia
Leah
Leda
Lee
Leila
Leilani
Lelia
Lemuela
Lena
Lenore
Leola
Leoma
Leona
Leonarda
Leontine
Leopoldine
Leota
Lesley
Leta
Letha
Letitia
Levina
Lexine
Liana
Libby
Lida
Lilac
Lilis
Lilith
Lillian
Lilybelle
Lina
Linda
Lindsey
Linette
Linnea
Lisa
Lisbeth
Livia
Lodema
Lois
Lola
Lona
Lora
Lorelei
Lorena
Lorraine
Lotus
Louise
Love
Luana
Lucille
Lucinda
Lucretia
Lucy
Ludella
Ludmilla
Luella
Luna
Lunetta
Lupe
Lurline

Luvena
Lydia
Lynn
Lyris
Lysandra

Mab
Mabel
Madeline
Madge
Madra
Magnolia
Mahala
Maia
Maida
Maisie
Majesta
Malca
Malina
Malinda
Malva
Malvina
Manuela
Mara
Marcella
Marcia
Marelda
Marella
Margaret
Marian
Maribel
Marigold
Marina
Maris
Marjorie
Marlene
Marmara
Martha
Martina
Marvel
Mary
Matilda
Mattea
Maude
Maureen
Mavis
Maxine
May
Meara
Medea
Megan
Mehitabel
Melanie
Melantha
Melba
Melina
Melinda
Melissa
Melody
Mercedes
Mercie
Mercy
Meredith
Merle
Merritt
Merry
Meta
Mia

Michelle
Mignon
Mildred
Millicent
Minerva
Minna
Mira
Mirabel
Miranda
Miriam
Modesty
Moira
Mona
Monica
Morgana
Morna
Moselle
Muriel
Musetta
Myra
Myrna
Myrtle

Nadine
Naida
Nancy
Naomi
Nara
Narda
Nata
Natalie
Nathania
Neala
Neda

Nelda
Nerine
Nerissa
Nevada
Nicole
Nike
Nila
Nina
Nissa
Nita
Noel
Nola
Noleta
Nolita
Nona
Nora
Norberta
Norma
Novia
Nunciata
Nydia
Nyssa

Obelia
Octavia
Odele
Odelia
Odessa
Odette
Ola
Olga
Olinda
Olive
Olympia

Oma
Ona
Ondine
Opal
Ophelia
Oralie
Orea
Oriana
Orna
Orpah
Orva

Page
Paige
Pallas
Palma
Pamela
Pandora
Panphila
Pansy
Panthea
Parthenia
Patience
Patricia
Paula
Peace
Pearl
Peggy
Pelagia
Penelope
Penthea
Peony
Pepita
Perdita
Perfecta
Pernella
Persis
Petra
Petula
Petunia
Phedra
Phenice
Philana
Philantha
Philberta
Philippa
Philomena
Philona
Phoebe
Phyllis
Pia
Pierrette
Pilar
Piper
Placida
Pomona
Poppy
Portia
Prima
Primavera
Primrose
Priscilla
Prudence
Prunella
Psyche

Quartas
Quenby

Quenna
Querdia
Quinta

Rachel
Radella
Rae
Raina
Ramona
Rana
Randy
Raphaela
Rebba
Rebecca
Regina
Rena
Renata
Rene
Renita
Reseda
Reva
Rexana
Rhea
Rhoda
Ria
Rica
Ricarda
Rima
Risa
Rita
Riva
Roanna
Roberta
Robin
Rochelle
Roderica
Rohana
Rolanda
Roma
Romilda
Romola
Ronalda
Rosabel
Rosalba
Roselinda
Rosamond
Rosanna
Rose
Rosemarie
Rosetta
Rowena
Roxane
Ruby
Rudelle
Rue
Rufina
Ruth

Saba
Sabina
Sabra
Sabrina
Sacha
Sadira
Salina
Salome
Salvia
Samantha

Samara
Samuela
Sancia
Sandra
Sapphire
Sarah
Sarita
Savanna
Scarlett
Sebastiana
Secunda
Sela
Selena
Selima
Selma
Semele
Senalda
Septima
Seraphina
Serena
Serilda
Sharon
Sheba
Sheena
Sheila
Shelah
Shelley
Sherry
Shirley
Shoshana
Sibyl
Sidonia
Sidra
Sigfreda
Simone
Sirena
Solita
Sondra
Sonia
Sophia
Sophronia
Sorcha
Spring
Stacey
Star
Stella
Stephanie
Storm
Sunny
Susan
Swanhilda
Sydelle
Sydney
Sylvia

Tabitha
Tacita
Talia
Talitha
Tallulah
Tama
Tamara
Tammy
Tansy
Tara
Tempest
Tertia
Tessa

Thaddea
Thais
Thalassa
Thea
Thecia
Theda
Thelma
Themis
Theodora
Theodosia
Theola
Theone
Theophila
Theora
Thera
Theresa
Thetis
Thirza
Thisbe
Thomasina
Thora
Thorberta
Thyra
Tiberia
Tiffany
Tilda
Timothea
Tita
Titania
Toby
Toni
Topaz
Tourmaline
Tracy
Trilby
Trina
Trinette
Trista
Trixie
Trudy
True
Tuesday
Tullia

Udele
Ula
Ulrica
Ulva
Una
Undine
Urania
Uria
Ursa
Ursel
Ursula
Uta

Vala
Valda
Valeda
Valentina
Valerie
Valonia
Valora
Vanessa
Vania

Vanora
Varina
Vashti
Veda
Vega
Velda
Velika
Velma
Velvet
Ventura
Venus
Vera
Verbena
Verda
Verena
Verna
Veronica
Vespera
Vesta
Victoria
Vida
Vidonia
Vigilia
Vignette
Vincentia
Vinita
Vinna
Violet
Virgilia
Virginia
Viridas
Vita
Vivian
Voleta

Wahkuna
Walda
Wallis
Wanda
Wanetta
Warda
Welcome
Wendelin
Wendy
Wenona
Wesla
Wilda
Wilfreda
Wilhelmina
Wilona
Winema
Winifred
Winola
Wynne

Xanthe
Xaviera
Xenia
Xylia
Xylona

Yedda
Yetta
Yolanda
Yseult
Yvonne

Zabrina
Zandra

Zara
Zea
Zebada
Zena
Zenobia
Zera
Zerelda
Zerlina
Zeta
Zillah
Zinnia
Zipporah
Zita
Zoe
Zora
Zuleika

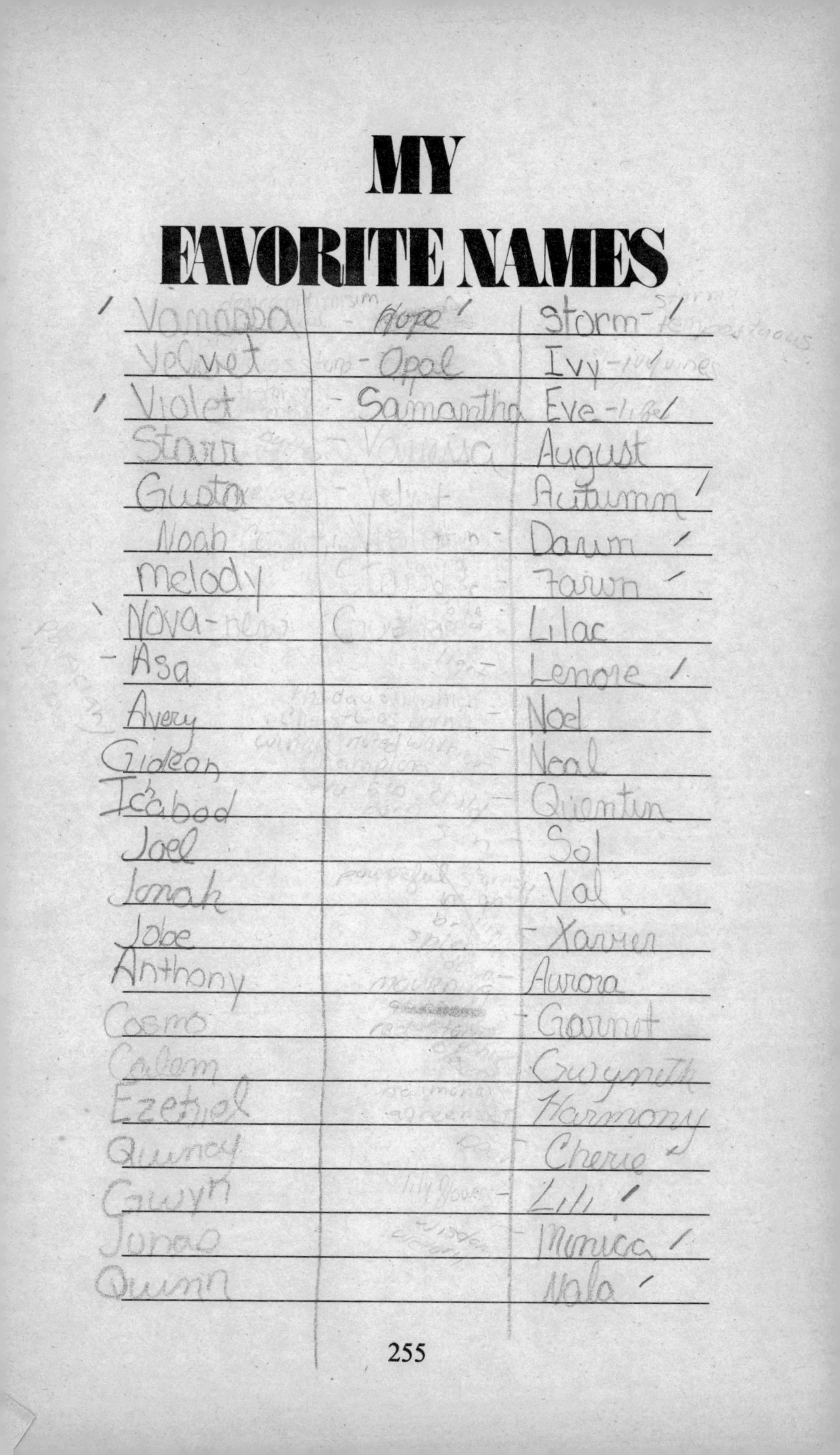

MY FAVORITE NAMES